PREPARING FOR CHRISTIAN MARRIAGE

An Inclusive Handbook for Straight and LGBTQ Couples Seeking a Joyful Marriage with Discussion Guide for Clergy

Dear Brother Jon
Fellow Laborer in Ministry
Steve R Wigall

Preparing for Christian Marriage
An Inclusive Handbook for Straight and LGBTQ Couples
Seeking a Joyful Marriage with Discussion Guide for Clergy
Author: The Rev. Steve R. Wigall, ThM, ThD

Published by: Canyonwalker Press
Reno, NV USA
www.CanyonWalkerPress.com

Cover design by: Andrea McNeeley
www.320.designs.com
Developmental Editor: Wendy Prell Danbury
Copy Editor: Elaine Bellamore Phillips

The Holy Bible, *English Standard Version*® (ESV®) is the primary
version used, without attribution, throughout all three sections of
Preparing for Christian Marriage. It is an excellent and faithful
modern translation. If a short phrase from a passage of Scripture
is quoted without attribution in the course of discussing a larger
passage of Scripture, the quoted words are taken from the ESV. In
addition, The Holy Bible, *Contemporary English Version*® (CEV®)
is cited several times, with attribution, because of its superior ability
to render the original Biblical languages in clear English sentences.

Library of Congress Control Number: 2016952188
ISBN: 978-1-61920-057-9

SYNOPSIS

Preparing for Christian Marriage is an inclusive and practical guide for couples like you, straight or LGBTQ, seeking to begin the joy-filled adventure of Christian Marriage. It is written in three parts. The first section for couples contains the text of a manual that spells out ten Biblical rules for a God blessed marriage. These rules describe the attitudes and actions that comprise *The Discipline of Family Love* the Scriptural goals for every Christian married couple. The implications of living out these loving goals are explained in six personal, pastoral care letters. These letters are designed for you as couples to read, and enjoy, and ponder. They are also designed for you to discuss with your church pastor. So, following each letter are discussion pages with questions guiding you and your pastor into a deeper look at the dynamics involved in the love-intensive and joy-filled work of building a Christian Marriage.

Section Two of *Preparing for Christian Marriage* is a Discussion Guide for your pastor to use in leading you through either three or six pre-marital lessons. You'll enjoy reading the letters and benefit from their pastoral care advice. But being able to discuss *The Discipline of Family Love* with your pastor, and gain his or her counsel, will make the Scripture's ten rules for married love become clearer and more alive. Your pastor can use this resource in working with you as an individual couple or in leading a couple's group for individuals preparing for Christian Marriage.

Section Three of *Preparing for Christian Marriage* is entitled, "With a Christ-like Love." This section is a study paper for you and your pas-tor to read on your own so you can go into the theology of Marriage from a Christian, Biblical, and Reformation point of view. This study paper takes you through the Christian rationale for civil Marriage Equality and Christian Marriage inclusivity. The overriding theme in this section is the affirmation that Christian Marriage is God's school where all couples are given the opportunity to learn to love each other with a Christ-like love.

iii

"It was a joy to read and so accessible. I especially liked the way the book was divided. The first section went through a thoughtful overview of the many facets of Christian marriage. Here and there, the discussion includes issues unique to gay couples, but the real emphasis is on Christian family and how it works. This is how I expect marriage will be approached in another 20 years – taking a sort of "orientation blind" approach. As part of an already-married couple, I looked at how some things discussed in this first section have turned out in my marriage, in my in-law relationships, for example, and in how I've tolerated and grown through our mutual differences.

"In the discussion sections, I thought the worksheets were laid out well. There were no rhetorical questions and no bias toward "the right" answer, so it leaves discussion open for different couples to arrive at different understandings. It is clearly something that will work in counseling either one couple or a group.

"I liked the fact that the theological foundation, which is something that still needs to be laid in our time, was in its own space at the end. The theological discussion of the civil marriage for gay citizens and Christian Marriage for gay Christian couples avoids being falsely inclusive by suggesting that "some of my best friends are..." or "we need to include even ...." I found that it also posed some deep questions about Scripture, and offered helpful suggestions for further thinking."

Marsha Stevens-Pino:
Founder and Director of BALM Ministries
Singer song-writer, "The Mother of Contemporary Christian Music," according to The Encyclopedia of Contemporary Christian Music

TABLE OF CONTENTS

SECTION 1

INTRODUCTION FOR COUPLES

A re you thinking about Christian Marriage? Welcome to my office; take a seat! It's nice to meet you; I want to get to know you better. And, as we work together, I want to help you get to know each other better. But first, let me introduce myself. I'm an ordained Presbyterian minister. A large part of my ministry experience has been devoted to the nurture and support of Christian couples. My wife and I spent over a decade involved in the ministry of Presbyterian Marriage Encounter – a ministry that focuses on the strengthening and enrichment of Christian Marriage. While doing that work, we served as the clergy couple on Marriage Encounter weekends around the country, as well as serving on both the national Presbyterian Marriage Encounter board, and on the American Interfaith Marriage Encounter governing board.

My wife and I were married in 1974; and I'd like to say we've been happily married ever since. But the truth is, although our marriage is happy today, we've had to battle our way through a fair share of struggle and conflict. No one could have told me in the beginning of my marriage how hard and painful it can be to learn to love another person, or finally, how richly rewarding it could become. Both are true.

I can't predict what struggles you two may experience as a couple. But *in the interest of full disclosure,* I can admit my wife and I faced a time when we thought the only answer for us was divorce. Our communication styles were so different that at times we were certain our every attempt to reach out to each other would result only in pain. We didn't consider divorce because we had given up on our marriage. We considered divorce because we were tired of hurting each other.

Graduate school was an experience that pulled us apart. Money and professional ups and downs have pulled and pried us apart. Illness, tiredness, and times when we were too stressed out to even try to communicate; all these have pulled at us and pitted us against each other. Many of these struggles have been painful. We even fought our way through couples' therapy. And yet, I'm ready to say the work of learning to love my wife was more than worth it. That's why I'm not afraid to start out our conversation by stating up front that marriage is hard. I want to assure you from my personal experience that the hard work of building a strong marriage is perhaps the most satisfying and joyful human accomplishment.

So, when I share with you what I've learned about marriage, from Scripture and from life experience, you can know I'm not speaking platitudes. I'm sharing hard-won insights and truths I've personally lived.

Since we're not actually sitting in my office, and since you're reading this discussion in book form, let me tell you the story of how this book came about. In one way or another, I've been writing this book in my mind for over four decades in conversations with couples and in conference venues. And although this is true, I didn't start out wanting to give marriage advice or teach the principles of Christian Marriage. For the first many years of my own marriage, I started out just trying as hard as I could to make my own marriage a happy one. I entered marriage thinking I knew exactly what I was in for; but over time, I found out I had a lot more to learn. What I've written in this book is the "more to learn" which I've discovered.

This book is about Christian Marriage, so you won't be surprised the story behind the book starts with my Christian faith and the Christian faith of my wife-to-be. We both grew up seeing ourselves as Christians, with Christian parents in Christian homes; and we entered marriage convinced we knew how to do it. We weren't cocky, or even falsely confident. We went through pre-marital counseling with two different ministers, one a good friend, and the second the minister who married us. We worked hard to discuss ahead of time and at length every marriage-related issue we could think of. We were motivated to get it right.

I want to give credit to you, the couples who are reading this book. You want to get it right, too. That's why you are thinking about Christian Marriage. Perhaps you grew up in a Christian family. Perhaps you are relatively new to the Christian faith. Perhaps you've always considered yourself to be Christian but haven't ever thought much about it. Or maybe you've grown up in a different faith tradition and are now considering Christian Marriage because you are planning to marry a Christian. I give you credit for thinking about building a marriage around Christian principles, and on Christian faith in God.

I also give you credit for taking marriage seriously. I don't know what kind of marriage your parents had, (if any). But I'm sure you know staying married is hard for many couples. You know a large percentage of couples don't make it. And you want to be among those do.

I further give you credit for *already* having strong convictions about what marriage means and what it will demand of you. I've never counseled a couple who hadn't *already* given it a lot of thought and talked with each other extensively about what their marriage will mean for them, about what they both want, and about what they both expect to give. So I credit you as a couple with taking your upcoming marriage seriously. I further give you both a lot of credit for being willing to challenge yourselves to go for more than a civil marriage, to give your hearts and minds to undertake a Christian Marriage which will involve learning to love each other with a Christ-like love. As you read through this book, engage in the exercises and participate in the discussions. You'll have the chance to get a deeper vision of Christian Marriage, and the Christ-like love it will ask you to learn.

Now, back to the story of this book. The year was 1990. I had departed from my first parish in New Jersey to enter doctoral studies at Boston University School of Theology. I was involved in the coursework phase of a *dual* emphasis Th.D. in both Psychology, emphasizing the psychology of religion; and in Theology, emphasizing the history of Christian Spirituality. My son was three years old. That year was the first time my wife and I began to discuss the possibility our son might be gay. Over the next twenty years, we kept our "ears to the ground," enjoying his childhood years, but knowing our son might be special in more ways than just being ours.

During these years, I was busy at many things. I was a church pastor in New Jersey. I was a Boston University theology student, working towards my Th.D. But perhaps my most important job during these years, I was a hands-on, stay-at-home house dad, raising my son. As a sideline to being a house dad, I did a lot of thinking and studying about how the young man my son would grow into might be both Christian and gay. I didn't know for sure my son would be gay. But it was important to me as a Christian dad and pastor, to be ready to advise and counsel him should he come to the realization, "Yes, I am gay."

I wanted to know, as my son's pastor and his parent, how to help him understand and accept his sexuality. I especially wanted to know how to help him become solidly rooted in his Christian faith. And appropriate to the topic of this book, I wanted to know how to prepare my son for being happily married. I wrote the first draft of the pamphlet for couples, contained in Section 1 of this work, to express the teaching and wisdom about Christian Marriage I wanted to pass on to my son.

You'll notice, as you read the statement of the biblical principles behind Christian Marriage which I've expressed in all three parts of this book, I make no reference to whether couples are same-sex or opposite-sex. There's an important reason for this. My study of Scripture, and theology (especially Protestant Reformation theology), has convinced me God's standard for Christian Marriage, and God's invitation to enter into Christian Marriage, is identical for both same- and opposite-sex couples.

For that reason, this book takes a strong biblical and theological stand in favor of Marriage Equality and full inclusion of same-sex couples in the life of the church. I firmly believe both Christian Marriage and a Christian understanding of civil marriage, should be based in a principled Marriage Equality stance. Both American society and the Christian church have the strongest reasons to offer marriage to same- and opposite-sex couples equally. To both on the same basis. To both on equal footing. Exactly the same civil marriage and exactly the same Christian Marriage. The reasons for this are made especially clear in Section 3 of this work. I hope you'll enjoy reading it.

The next event in the story of this book's development took place at a meeting of the Presbytery of Northern New England (PCUSA) – the presbytery to which I belong as a Christian minister. I believe the year was 2010, in the fall. By this time, I had been thinking for roughly twenty years about how people might be both Christian and gay. And I had been thinking about the marriage counsel I would give my son. He was in his sophomore year of college and had finally come out to himself and to us as his parents. After long years of parental studying, waiting, watching, and wondering, our guessing about his sexual orientation was finally over. For the first time we were able to start talking with our son about what it means for him to be gay and about his hopes and dreams for his own marriage and family. We were even able to have conversations about dating. It was kind of funny. In the same way parents can harass their sons to find a "nice girl," as his parents, we could now give our son friendly harassment to find a "nice guy."

At that 2010 meeting, my presbytery was discussing how to help pastors who wanted to begin ministering to same-sex couples. No pastoral resource material existed at that time. Presbyterian ministers were not yet officially permitted by our denomination to marry same-sex Christian couples. Today in 2016, not only do the four New England states in our presbytery (MA, ME, NH and VT) all permit same-sex marriage, but the Supreme Court has made Marriage Equality the law in all 50 states. Our denomination has now given ministers the right to perform same-sex Christian Marriage. But in 2010, although two of these four states permitted same-sex marriage, our denomination would not allow us to officiate.

Even though we could not officiate, many of the Presbyterian ministers with whom I had talked had young gay family members, or knew close friends with gay children. They longed to find a way to include these young men and women in the fellowship of Presbyterian families as well as in the fellowship of Christian married couples. They longed to include them even in the fellowship of married couples with children. Many of us ministers, and I counted myself among them, wanted to embrace the ministry opportunities which Marriage Equality would bring to our denomination. In my heart, I felt torn by the anguish experienced by the many Christian families with gay children, families being torn apart and wounded deeply by the church's hostile attitude towards their gay sons and daughters.

So, at its fall 2010 meeting, when my presbytery acted to establish a committee to prepare resource materials for pastors, I volunteered to serve. Being elected to this committee gave me an official reason to start writing down everything I had thought and learned on the subject. I set right to work on a pamphlet for couples. I saw this as an opportunity to serve my church, its pastors, and its families. My son was set to graduate from college in a couple of years and I wanted to have the marriage pamphlet ready to give him as a graduation gift. Then as I finished the first draft of the pamphlet for couples, I started work on a Study Paper for pastors. I began to ask myself what I'd want to tell my fellow pastors to help give them a framework for the new ministry of Marriage Equality.

I hope you read and enjoy Section 3 of this work. It's the Study Paper I wrote for my fellow pastors. Because I want you to enjoy reading Section 3, I'm not going to include any spoilers in this introduction. But I'm going to let you in on two of the happiest discoveries I made while writing it. I found New Testament Scripture redefines Christian Marriage giving it a more profound spiritual meaning than the procreative meaning suggested by Old Testament Scripture. The New Testament defines Christian Marriage as a relationship of faithful, self-sacrificial love, based on the model of Christ and the church; instead of a procreative relationship, based on the model of Adam and Eve. Consequently, a Christian Marriage can be made up by either an opposite-sex relationship or a same-sex couple. Section 3 examines the scriptural evidence for this.

I was also happy to discover that Reformed theology, contained in the Presbyterian confessions, provides a moral framework for same-sex civil marriage and same-sex Christian Marriage. Presbyterian theology is very clear that the moral framework for marriage applies equally for straight couples and gay couples. In fact, God's moral guidance is the same for all people and especially for all Christians. God's complete moral guidance to humanity is contained in the Ten Commandments which God gave to Moses. For straight couples and gay couples, God's moral guidance is the same. Be sexually faithful to your partner in marriage (Exodus 20:14). Don't sexually objectify your marriage partner with the lust that sees them as something you can own or use (Exodus 20:17). You can read a full discussion of these moral principles in Parts One and Three.

My hope and plan is the two of you will take part in the discussion activities provided for in Section 2. Your parish pastor or Christian Educator will lead you through either three discussion sessions or six discussion sessions. Section 2 represents another part of my story – the teacher part. My daddy insisted, that after college, I earn a teaching credential. So after I graduated from the University of California with my bachelor's degree, I completed an education degree. I never used my teacher skills in a public classroom; but I've used these skills constantly in the church, developing curriculum and teaching classes for both youth and adults. Teaching and learning is one of my greatest life joys; and I anticipate you as a couple will enjoy the discussions.

You're holding the result of the book story in your hands. But there's another part of my personal story I want to share. Right after our son came out to us, he began to tell us about his positive experiences with his gay student organization at the University of Maine. His stories helped me realize I needed to do some serious catching up. My awareness of the LGBTQ movement needed to be updated. A new generation of LGBTQ folks had come along, forming the Rainbow Movement, and taking over from the Gay Pride Movement I remembered from the 1960's. New things were going on, and I needed to update my awareness.

I wasn't going back to college to involve myself in a gay student group. But I did some research, and I found the Gay Christian Network (GCN). GCN is an online support group for LGBTQ Christians. I joined, and began to meet young gay Christians as well as gay Christians of my own age. I realized quickly GCN was filling an important ministry need for these Christian brothers and sisters. Many had been orphaned by their churches. Many had been emotionally and spiritually abused by their churches. And most had simply never been lovingly pastored or carefully nurtured in the faith. I don't mean I was meeting people with whom I didn't agree. I mean I was meeting people who were afraid God didn't love them, who were plagued by feelings of guilt and shame, but who still loved God even though they had been alienated from their church homes.

Being a pastor-person at heart and by training, I began to reach out to my fellow GCN members. In my mind, I began to accept GCN as a new ministry challenge. It wasn't long before I became a volunteer Moderator and started to more officially minister to other members. I have to say my involvement in GCN has been an eye-opening and mind-expanding experience. Yes, I've met a lot of wounded people. But every church has wounded people. My biggest surprise and delight has come from observing the deep spirituality and care with which members of GCN minister to each other's faith struggles and encourage each other in the midst of the emotional crises so many experience.

I've written *Preparing for Christian Marriage* for Christian couples like you, whether you are gay or straight. I welcome you to let this study and discussion of Christian Marriage deepen and enrich your awareness of the Christ-like love which is the lifeblood of Christian Marriage. In the spirit of GCN, I'm not defining the meaning of being Christian in partisan denominational terms. My own faith perspective, from which I'm writing, is the perspective of the Reformation redis-covery of the New Testament gospel. But I'm defining the meaning of Christian faith inclusively to be faith in God as shaped by God's self-revelation in Jesus Christ. I consider this faith to be a reality in which you and I can continue to grow as long as we live. My prayer is that reading this book and participating in its discussion exercises, will be an enriching experience for you.

I've learned from my involvement in the GCN community that many gay Christians come to Christianity with an almost crippling set of faith struggles. These are not completely different from the difficulties straight Christians face: guilt, shame, fear, doubt. But I want to acknowledge the likelihood that many gay couples who are reading this book have been targeted for abuse and attack by their churches. I can't address every faith question which gay couples may have. But I can lay out a simple summary of my pastoral counsel.

Pastoral counsel. Guilt and shame involve fear and have no place in a Christian's relationship with God. When we understand God's love for us, we no longer have any reason to fear God or God's judgment.

> **By this is love perfected with us, so that we may have confidence for the day of judgment. . . . There is no fear in love, but perfect love casts out fear. For fear has to do with punishment, and whoever fears has not been perfected in love. (I John 4:17-18)**

God wants us to come to him with confidence. If our hearts condemn us we should remember, that God knows everything about us, realizing our weakness better than we do, and does not condemn us.

> **By this we shall know that we are of the truth and reassure our heart before him; for whenever our heart condemns us, God is greater than our heart, and he knows everything. Beloved, if our heart does not condemn us, we have confidence before God. (I John 3:19-21)**

> **There is therefore now no condemnation for those who are in Christ Jesus. (Romans 8:1)**

The forgiveness and acceptance we have from God are complete, covering our every sin, and encompassing our whole lives.

> **In him we have redemption through his blood, the forgiveness of our trespasses, according to the riches of his grace. (Ephesians 1:7)**

> **And you, who were dead in your trespasses and the uncircumcision of your flesh, God made alive together with him, having forgiven us all our trespasses. (Colossians 2:13)**

> **All this is from God, who through Christ reconciled us to himself and gave us the ministry of reconciliation; that is, in Christ God was reconciling the world to himself, not counting their trespasses against them, and entrusting to us the message of reconciliation. (2 Corinthians 5:18-19)**

I say to my gay brothers and sisters, neither gay nor straight sexual orientation makes any difference to God who creates us. The sexuality with which we are born is covered by God's Creation blessing: "It is good!" As I already explained, God's moral standards for his gay and straight children are the same. Be sexually faithful; and avoid lust that sexually objectifies your partner. You will have the chance to discuss these moral standards and their implications during your sessions with your pastor.

This completes my self-introduction. I've related a little about my life experience and how that experience has shaped my values on the subject of Christian Marriage. More than anything, I want you two to weather the rigors of marriage and discover its joys. That desire has been in my mind the entire time as I composed this work and completed putting it together. The challenge of Christian Marriage is to learn to love with a Christ-like love: faithful and self-sacrificial. No other challenge is greater. No other challenge has the potential of yielding you richer rewards.

Warmly in Christ,

The Rev. Steve R. Wigall, Th.M., Th.D.

Lawrence, Massachusetts

How irreverent are the stiff and stuffy!
Who is less Godly than those who reject joy and laughter?
Who dishonors the Creator more than those who refuse to be earthy?
How wild and beautiful our God – who is in love with all creation
and every person!
Who can keep God's love from healing human hearts with celestial
laughter and joy?

Couples' Pamphlet: Preparing for Christian Marriage

Are You Thinking About Christian Marriage?

". . . Yes, we are. We love each other and want to spend our lives together. Isn't that what Christian Marriage *is all about*?"

It is. Christian Marriage is a faithful, loving relationship between two people who commit to being life partners. That *is* what *it's all about* – that . . . and *so much more*.

Christian Marriage *Is All About* . . . Family

Christian Marriage is a good thing. It makes families, and family is both one of God's best blessings and most difficult disciplines. Accepting Christian Marriage means accepting the blessing and *The Discipline of Family Love*.

Christians strongly believe in the importance of family. Family relationships give shape, strength, and purpose to the lives of children as they grow towards maturity. In family relationships, children learn to love, to think of others, and to make a difference for good in the world. Family relationships are part of *The Discipline of Family Love*.

When we mature as individuals, we leave our fathers and mothers and may seek a life partner with whom we can join to create families of our own. In these new families, we hope to find and share the companionship and support all people need. Joining with a life partner is also part of *The Discipline of Family Love*.

Christian Marriage *Is All About* . . . Learning to Love

The Discipline of Family Love is both joyous and vexing because it involves us in relationships that confront us with life's greatest blessings and life's greatest difficulties. God intends for us to grow in our ability to love through being enriched by the blessings of family love and strengthened by its difficulties.

Starting a new family by marrying a life partner is not the only way to learn the lessons of love. Singleness is also a normal part of human life. All married people begin life by being single, and may become single again, if their marriage ends. Many people are single for a lifetime. Fortunately, God can bring all the blessing and discipline of love into the lives of people who find themselves single, or, who choose to remain single.

However, God ***commonly*** brings the discipline of love into human life through marriage and family. God even encourages people to look for a life partner whom they can marry and work with to create a new family. Christian Marriage is a good thing; but it offers neither a magic ticket to human happiness, nor guarantees the new family a couple creates will be perfectly loving.

Christians believe sin permeates the world and damages the human ability to form relationships – including family relationships. Consequently, accepting Christian Marriage means accepting learning *The Discipline of Family Love* will be an ongoing, and sometimes uphill, lifetime struggle.

Christian Marriage *Is All About* . . . Living in Community. The presence of sin in the world means no one comes to Christian Marriage with a perfect experience of family love. It also means that married couples can expect creating a loving family will require a lifetime of work.

Consequently, every Christian family needs the support of the Christian faith community to help it handle *The Discipline of Family Love*. As all Christian people are welcome at Christ's communion table, and none are to be excluded; so all Christian families are welcome in the supportive communion of Christ's church, and none are to be excluded.

When we accept Christian Marriage and become a Christian family, we will be called to reach out to and support other families in the church community. In return, we should expect the welcome of church families and be prepared to receive their support.

Clearly, Christian Marriage is *so much more* than a relationship between two people who love each other and want to spend their lives together. But exactly what does the *so much more* of Christian Marriage ask couples to *do*?

Christian Marriage asks couples to accept *The Discipline of Family Love*. For couples, this means taking the following actions and living by the following values, all of which find their basis in the teaching of Scripture.

1. Be faithful to the one you love.

Do not betray the one you love by being sexually unfaithful to them.

(Exodus 20:14)

2. Do not "lust after" the one you love.

This means: do not violate the one you love by sexually objectifying or using them.

(Exodus 20:17; Matthew 5:28; James 1:14)

3. Treat the one you love as sacred.

When we realize people are sacred to God, we learn to treat ourselves and each other as sacred. That is why we neither sexually violate nor betray ourselves or each other.

(1 Corinthians 6:15-19)

4. Realize that married sex is God-blessed.

All human relationships are infected by sin including every human sexual relationship. The Good News is, when married couples love each other, as does God – with a faithful love (like Christ's love for the church), their sexual relationship has God's blessing. God wants to free married couples from any idea their sex lives are evil, or dirty, or anything but God-blessed.

(Romans 3:10 – 18, Ephesians 5:21 – 33, Hebrews 13:4)

5. Be unashamed of your loving feelings and affection.

When the love between two people is vibrant and healthy, they neither desire to hide their love from friends, nor want to withdraw themselves from society – either out of shame or guilt or out of a desire for secrecy. They are proud and unashamed to express their feelings of love.

(Song of Solomon 8:1)

6. Involve the one you love in your family.

Married love is not just a private matter between two people. At its heart, it involves expanding family ties and extending the reach of a family's love to include new people. Couples need to share their lives and their love with members of their extended families.

(Song of Solomon 8:2)

15

7. Find ways to give creative expression to your love.

All families need to find ways to express their love. This can involve parenting children and nurturing social causes. It certainly will involve giving support to, and receiving support from, other families in the Christian faith community.

(Psalms 128:3; I Corinthians 12:24-26; Romans 16:10-11; I Peter 4:9)

8. Learn how to love someone who is different.

It is natural to be drawn to a life partner who has supplementary and even opposite personality characteristics. Christian Marriage challenges life partners to embrace each other with the kind of love that values and treasures a person for the ways in which they are different. See Isaiah 55:8-9, which says, "My thoughts are not your thoughts, neither are your ways my ways, declares the Lord."

9. Expect love to provoke you to grow and change.

Persons different enough to fascinate us and win our love may provoke and even infuriate us. A life partner will do more than complete us with strengths we need – but do not have. They will also provoke us to deal with issues we need to face – but want to avoid.

(Ephesians 4:26)

10. Strive to build a lasting love relationship.

Commit yourself to building a lasting love relationship that treasures its first joy; seeks understanding and reconciliation when there is conflict; admits when its actions cause hurt; takes pleasure in mutual self-revelation; and does all it can to foster an enduring bond of honesty and trust.

Concluding Questions and Answers about Christian Marriage

Q. How does a couple enter into Christian Marriage?

A. Christian Marriage begins when two people promise before God to love each other exclusively for as long as they live and express their commitment through sexual union. Christian Marriage is consecrated when the church celebrates the joining of these two lives through a Christian wedding which publicly recognizes their place as a married couple within the Christian faith community.

Q. What is the essence of Christian Marriage?

A. The essential and defining characteristic of Christian Marriage is a commitment between two people to love each other faithfully for a lifetime.

Q. What is the difference between Christian Marriage and civil marriage?

A. Christian Marriage is the spiritual union of two people which is recognized by God and validated by the Christian Church. Civil marriage is a legal partnership between two people which meets the requirements for marriage according to the laws of the state in which the couple resides.

Q. Who may enter into Christian Marriage?

A. The many blessings of Christian Marriage belong to any couple who shows they want those blessings by willingly accepting all The Disciplines of Family Love.

Q. What is the purpose of Christian Marriage?

A. The blessings of Christian Marriage are an essential part of God's plan for human life. At its best, Christian Marriage:

☐ Embodies the characteristics of God's love,

- ☐ Is a means through which God transforms a couple into Christ-likeness, and

- ☐ Offers the promise of human fulfillment to a couple and their community.

(Genesis 1:26-28; Exodus 34:6; 1 John 4:16; 2 Corinthians 3:18)

Thoughts you want to discuss, and questions you want to ask:

Lesson One:

Personal Letter to Couples

Dear Precious Couples,

It's really nice to talk again. This will be your first discussion session. I've already had a chance to introduce myself. Now we get to delve into the good stuff, the meaning of Christian Marriage. I'm not going to pre-empt the pastor or the Christian Educator with whom you'll be meeting; but I want to share with you some of my personal convictions behind the themes in Lesson One.

You may wonder why this first lesson emphasizes the importance of family. You are undoubtedly most conscious of the blossoming of the love between you that has bound you together as a couple. If this is a second marriage for either of you, and your upcoming marriage will create a blended family, then family is very likely in the forefront of your minds. If not, family may seem like a second, third, or even fourth level concern. If you are a gay couple, or are getting married later in life past a point where you are interested in childbirth or child rearing, you may be aware of the considerable social pressure to define your marriage in terms of children. A gay couple may even have felt the condemnation of churches who believe a marriage is only legitimate if it produces children. In the face of these pressures, some of you may have looked inward and focused more on your couple love than on family love. And, if your in-laws have been less than supportive, then you may have had even more reason to focus inward.

I'm starting our exploration of Christian Marriage by discussing family love because I want us to talk about what your family owes you, and what you will owe your children, if you have them. I believe as strongly as possible that when a couple has children, they make several implied promises to them. I'm suggesting there is an unwritten contract between parents and their children. This contract usually expresses itself in the way parents give their children affection, provide for their children's physical needs, train them, and include their children in the life of the family. It is your parent's desire to include you in the life of your family that I want to talk about.

Let me be direct. Whether your parents do this or not, they should welcome your marriage as an extension of their family. They should embrace your children as their grandchildren. The implied promise your parents made at your birth was to give you the right to build a marriage that extends their family. To say it simply, your parents promised to welcome you and your partner, as a couple, into their family life and family activities. Expect them to have you over and to share family holidays with you: birthdays, Thanksgiving, Christmas, New Year's, and any other family gathering. Expect your parents and your partner's parents to want to include you as a married couple in their family life. In the same way, if you have children, expect to welcome into your family the partners whom your children choose.

I'm aware not every couple reading this book will have positive parent and in-law experiences. If both sets of in-laws are welcoming and supportive, you will be blessed. But it's possible that neither set of in-laws will be welcoming. It's possible just one set of in-laws will be welcoming. It's possible that you as a couple will enjoy one set of in-laws more. One young woman whose marriage I performed found down the road her husband was habitually unfaithful. A silver lining for her was the positive and supportive relationship she had developed with her in-laws.

Your partner's family may not only be a great support in tough times; they may also turn out to be a source of helpful insider information. His or her parents, and perhaps brothers or sisters, will have seen your partner in all their moods and observed all their tricks. Your in-laws may help you understand your partner and figure out how to get them out of a funk or to help them through a tough emotional patch. On a lighter note, in-laws can be a delightful source of tease-worthy stories which you might not otherwise get to hear. Brothers and sisters get to tease each other because they know these family tales. Hang out with your in-laws, keep your ears open, and you'll likely hear a good number of gems involving your partner.

So, let me encourage the two of you to cultivate a good relationship with your in-laws for yourselves and for the children you may have. This might not always be possible, but at this early stage of your relationship, you might not see why in-law relationships are so valuable. I suggest it will be clearer to you if you think of your marriage as not just launching a couple love but as launching a new family which is an organic part of two families – yours and your partner's.

Let me make another personal observation. Couples just starting out may need to work harder to build in-law relationships. Or the opposite might be true. One or the other of you may be too emotionally close to their parents. Getting married is about transferring your primary love from your parents to your marriage partner. Talking about this with each other can be tricky. There can be hurt feelings and arguments over the perception one of you is too emotionally tied to their parents or the opinion that one is spending too much time with their parents. My wife and I both struggled with this problem.

I'm not going to share with you the details of the couples' therapy we received; but I'll suggest one thing. Try to create enough emotional distance from each set of parents to help you shift from a parent-child relationship to a shared couple relationship. This means you will be ambassador and spokesperson for your spouse. It also means your spouse will be your ambassador and spokesperson. Defend each other; stand up for each other; speak up for each other's good points. Build your own relationship with your in-laws. But increasingly learn to relate to both sets of in-laws as a couple.

Another aspect of family love is family values. I confess the church has often oversimplified and distorted the meaning of family values. By incorrectly assuming Christian Marriage is all about procreation, the church has too often defined family values in terms of an opposite-sex pairing that results in bearing children. The meaning of marriage and family is far more complex and wonderful than the ability to give birth to children. If you are a same-sex couple, regardless of whether or not you want children, or if you are a childless opposite-sex couple, you can embrace the family values of a Christian Marriage. A childless couple, adoptive parents, and a couple with a dozen children – all can be Christian Marriages.

A Christian Marriage has great value because it accepts the challenge of embodying a Christ-like love exemplified in the love between Christ and the church. That love is self-sacrificial and faithful. This means you put the needs of your partner ahead of your own, and you live a life of sexual faithfulness. The meaning of being sexually faithful is pretty clear, but balancing your needs and your partner's is a constantly shifting task. Sometimes your needs will be to the fore. Sometimes your partner's needs will be first. Ideally, both of your needs will grow over time to become couple needs. As you grow in couple love, you will both want to learn to strive to meet each other's needs and desires. You will learn to be honest with your partner about what you need and want. You will also learn to enjoy discovering your partner's needs and wants and meeting them as much as you enjoy having your own met.

What you cannot do is meet all your partner's needs. Love will motivate you to try; but life won't let you succeed. Similarly, your partner won't be able to meet all your needs. It would be a mistake for you to expect him or her to live up to such an impossibly high standard. "All you need is love," makes a stellar song lyric. But it's not really fair to expect a wonderful love relationship to meet your every need. An important part of couple love is its ability to offer us support even when we feel the pinch of life's frustrations. Life is hard; it is a struggle. So is love. Love doesn't remove the struggle, but, it can make the struggle well worth it.

The self-sacrificial love between Christian Marriage partners enables both to become strong and unique individuals who increasingly take responsibility for meeting their own needs. It doesn't transform or merge them into a kind of a spiritual "single cell" unit. In much the same way, becoming one with Christ, or one with fellow Christians in the body of Christ, doesn't jeopardize our individuality. Our involvement in these important Christian love relationships strengthens our individuality by teaching us to work towards meeting our needs through our involvement in these relationships.

Another primary value Christian Marriage embraces is equality. Just as Scripture says Christians are one in Christ and equal, so partners in Christian Marriage are one and equal, or as Paul says, they are *one flesh*. Your desire to put your partner first reaches out to your partner's desire to put you first. And self-sacrificial love reaches out in the spirit of equality to transform both your needs into shared needs. As you work at this Christ-like way of loving, you will experience two sets of competing needs less and less; more and more you will experience couple needs. *You and I* will become *us and we*.

At the same time, both of you will become even stronger as separate individuals. That is the mystery of Christ-like love. It creates unity and distinctness. It combines two people without merging them. It creates both one and two – togetherness without confusion. If you wonder what is uniquely Christian about this kind of love, I suggest you read the Athanasian Creed (ca. A.D. 500) on the subject of the Trinity. God is One; and each person of God is separate. In God, there is unity and distinctness. God's persons are not confused and not merged. God is oneness in eternal love. Christian Marriage aspires to a human love that copies Trinitarian love, a love that empowers marriage partners to experience both unity and distinctness.

23

Yes, procreation is a wonderful gift God gives to humanity. And the gift of children is a wonderful blessing that either same-sex or opposite-sex couples can give to society. But the more profound gift your Christian Marriage will give the world is the Christ-like love you will live out in the midst of daily life and struggles. Don't worry. Even as you read these words you surely realize you won't live up to this lofty standard.

The apostle Paul describes Christian Marriage as a mystery (Ephesians Chapter 5). He says it's primarily about the love between Christ and the church. I have a smile on my face as I write this; for Christ, this love isn't a mystery. It's natural for him to love this way. For us humans, this love remains a mystery. It's a love we can aspire to. It's a love we can struggle toward. Do we ever fully understand or attain it? Surely not. I smile again as I think how many times I've heard that straight couples are fit for Christian Marriage, while gay couples are not. Whether gay or straight, we are all human. I've got to point out that whoever undertakes Christian Marriage has an equal chance to fall short of the love it requires. There is no sexual orientation that gives anyone a *head start* or a *leg up* on loving like Christ. Yet that is the challenge and the opportunity Christian Marriage presents to you as a couple. Be excited, be afraid, and be thrilled by the possibilities that await you.

You'll notice in the couple pamphlet, *Preparing for Christian Marriage*, and in your discussions with your pastor or Christian Educator, you'll hear the phrase: *The Discipline of Family Love*. Let me explain why I describe love as a discipline. Our American culture has such a deeply ingrained fixation on romantic love. It's wonderful emotion, romantic love. It is one of the emotional icings on the cake of marriage. It's not the only icing; but it's one of the more delightful ones. However, love is way more than an emotion. Love is the daily choice to give yourself to another person. Love is choice, and action, and determination, and courage. Love is a whole person kind of thing. It is about giving the gift of your whole self; and learning to receive the gift of your lover's whole self. It begins with the choice to say, "I do," to someone special. And it requires you every day of your life to keep choosing to say, "I do."

You'll read in the pamphlet and you'll discuss during these sessions, the 10 disciplines of family love. I'm not going into all 10 here. But I want to briefly tell you about two disciplines that are daily essentials for keeping love alive. The first one you could call a happy discipline. It begins with taking joy in each other. At the outset of love, this is easy. You wouldn't be together if you didn't enjoy each other. You might think enjoying each other isn't a discipline. But it is. It can be easy to enjoy the ways you two are similar. But think about how it felt to live alone. Think about your longing to find that someone special who isn't you. And now you've found him or you've found her. And deep down, you're so excited. You know that this person is special. This one is different. Now it's time to start enjoying those differences.

You can think of being married like joining a fan club. You're going to stand up before God and a judge or pastor and say, "I do," to being your spouse's number-one fan. You'll collect memorabilia. You'll practice clapping and cheering. You'll study the little things non-fans won't ever know. And you'll be sure not to root and celebrate in silence. You'll tell your partner how much you enjoy them – daily. It's at this point the discipline comes in. You'll work to find fun ways to tell your partner about your deep enjoyment of their presence in your life. And you'll start learning to enjoy the ways you are different from each other. There will be things that are important to your partner which are not important to you. But for the sake of love, you'll learn to find them important, learn to appreciate them, and remember to cheer and clap like a devoted fan – every day.

My wife is a gardener and quilter. I'm not interested in doing either. But I've learned a whole bunch about flowers, which ones bloom in which seasons, heirloom vegetables, tomato stakes, and the best tomato varieties for New England weather. I've learned about quilting patterns, the difference between hand and machine stitching, which materials make good quilts and which don't, the art of combining colors and patterns, and even a little about the history of quilting as an American folk art. I've learned to cheer for the garden each year and to enjoy cooking with garden-grown vegetables. I'm a beneficiary of my wife's garden. And I try to remember to say I appreciate the work she puts into digging in the dirt. I've learned to have opinions about quilt patterns and fabrics. At night, a blanket might keep me just as warm; but I've learned I'm blessed to sleep under quilts. My wife is a generous person who makes quilts as gifts, and I've learned to compliment the beautiful quilted gifts she gives, as well as the outstanding quilts she's made for our family.

There is a second discipline which is a daily essential to keeping love alive. We might call this the difficult discipline. It's about more than learning to enjoy your partner's differences. It's about the ways you and your partner irritate and even infuriate each other. Let's hope you don't infuriate each other on a daily basis. But the skill of handling anger and working towards reconciliation is a daily essential. Let me make an important observation. The happiness of your marriage will be less about how well you make love and more about how well you can express your anger and achieve reconciliation.

You will find an essential part of loving someone is dealing with hurt feelings and the anger that they kick up. Even for the two of you this will be true. When you lower your defenses to let your lover come in close, you let them get near enough to touch your most vulnerable feelings. They get near enough, like a sharp stone in your shoe, to cause both irritation and hurt. How you work through your angry feelings, and how to resolve your hurt feelings, will become a major part of your effort to build a strong and happy marriage.

Every one of us comes into marriage with the emotional wounds life has inflicted on us. Your marriage partner won't set out on purpose to step on your tender and bruised feelings. But your hurt feelings will have a way of inserting themselves at the most unexpected and awkward times. Handling anger and hurt will be as important to your marriage as sharing joy. Later, in these exercises, we'll have a chance to discuss some biblically based tools for dealing with these hard emotions.

We've talked about how *The Discipline of Family Love* includes developing and passing on family values. We've stated Christian family values are more profound than simply ensuring couples are opposite sex – and capable of procreation. Now I want to talk with you about the family values Christian Marriages can bring to their societies. Every Christian Marriage is a civil marriage when it has legal standing in state contract law. For that reason, beyond often being a vehicle for producing children and beyond being a vehicle for demonstrating Christ-like love, marriages also embody important social values.

For example, the very structure of marriage and family will force you and your partner to live together cooperatively and to work together economically. Living together as a family not only brings cooperation and work into your lives as a couple; it means you become an asset to your broader society. You become an embodiment of teamwork and industry. Industriousness is an essential family value because families need to work to support themselves. Families whose adult members work at jobs that are more productive, not only survive, they are also able to thrive.

Families not only encourage economic productivity, they force people to think of those with whom they work in close proximity. I expect your new family will develop a spirit of teamwork. And I envision your family team developing a strong sense of respect for each team member, for their dignity, and for each team member's rights – including the rights of children. I expect you to become a strong family which maintains its values but doesn't just look inward. Because your family will live within a neighborhood and a community, I anticipate you learning to care about your communities and wanting to make your communities better places to live – for yourselves and for others. I expect your family will develop the values of community concern and community service including the value of making a difference for good in the world.

The social structure of family life will uniquely enable your family to develop and inculcate so many values that promote the strength of society. The point is that you two may be entering marriage with eyes only for each other. Most days you probably don't look much farther than your couple relationship. What I'd like you to be aware of in this first lesson is, by getting married, you are starting a family, whether you have children or not, whether you adopt or not, whether you involve yourselves in the lives of your community's children or not. You will be a family. And as a family, you will be an asset to your church and to your community. Your church may not let you know; and your community may not let you know. But I'm going to say to you: Congratulations!

Warmly in Christ,

Steve

The Rev. Steve R. Wigall, Th.M., Th.D.

Lawrence, Massachusetts

How irreverent are the stiff and stuffy!
Who is less Godly than those who reject joy and laughter?
Who dishonors the Creator more than those who refuse to be earthy?
How wild and beautiful our God – who is in love with all creation
and every person!
Who can keep God's love from healing human hearts with celestial
laughter and joy?

LESSON ONE

DISCUSSION QUESTIONS

Class Opening

> (Leader) Gracious God, (pray in unison) **teach us to love each other as a couple with a Christ-like love. Teach us to know each other as Christ knows us. Teach us to take joy in each other as Christ takes joy in us.**
>
> **When love gets hard, let us be patient with each other as you are patient. Let us strive to be understanding as you understand. Let us be faithful to each other as you are faithful.**
>
> **Grant that through our shared successes and failures, through our shared happiness and sorrow, we might find lasting joy in the lessons of love which you teach us. We pray in the name of Jesus Christ, who shows us your love, calls us to love, and empowers us with your love. Amen**

Are You Thinking About Christian Marriage? . . .

". . . Yes, we are. We love each other and want to spend our lives together. Isn't that what Christian Marriage *is all about*?"

It is. Christian Marriage is a faithful, loving relationship between two people who commit to being life partners. That *is* what *it's all about* – that . . . and *so much more*.

Class Overview

29

Questions to discuss:

1. What questions do you have from the Couple's Pamphlet or from the Couple's Letter(s)?

2. How do you feel about the following definition? Christian Marriage can be defined as a faithful, loving relationship between two people who commit to being life partners.

3. What might distinguish Christian Marriage from civil marriage? Respond to the following three affirmations. (We will be discussing them further during this study.):

    a. A Christian Marriage creates FAMILY.

    b. A Christian Marriage teaches LOVE.

    c. A Christian Marriage teaches LIFE IN COMMUNITY.

Christian Marriage *Is All About* . . . Family.

Christian Marriage is a good thing. It makes families; and family is both one of God's best blessings and most difficult disciplines. Accepting Christian Marriage means accepting the blessing and *The Discipline of Family Love.*

Questions to discuss:

4. Do you agree with the following observation? In romantic relationships, we are commonly attracted to individuals different enough from us to fascinate us, disappoint us, get under our skin, and anger us.

5. Celebrating and enjoying your partner's similarities and differences is one of love's greatest blessings. Learning to work through your anger and your emotional wounds with a partner is one of love's greatest difficulties. How do you feel about taking on both love's blessings and difficulties?

6. Respond to the following observation. When we let someone close enough to us to love us, we let them close enough to both bless us and hurt us.

Christians strongly believe in the importance of family. Family relationships give shape, strength, and purpose to the lives of children as they grow towards maturity. In family relationships, children learn to love, to think of others, and to make a difference for good in the world. Family relationships are part of *The Discipline of Family Love*.

Questions to discuss:

7. It is important for couples seeking marriage to think about the values their new family will stand for. Each individual make a list of no more than five values you'd like your new family to uphold. Share and compare your lists.

8. Respond to the statement: Christian families will want to model for, and impart to their children, the citizenship values of cooperation, teamwork, respect for each person's dignity, a commitment to uphold human rights (and children's rights), and community service.

9. Respond to the statement: Christian families will want to model for and impart to their children the Christian value of an open acceptance of all persons, especially Christian persons – regardless of race, gender, age, or sexual orientation. (See Galatians 6:10)

10. What do you think might be the hardest part of developing the social grace within your family of warmly accepting both heterosexual and same-sex couples and families in your home and in your church fellowship?

When we mature as individuals, we leave our fathers and mothers and may seek a life partner with whom we can join to create families of our own. In these new families, we hope to find and share

31

the companionship and support which all people need. Joining with a life partner is also part of *The Discipline of Family Love*.

Questions to discuss:

11. Courtship is an important part of the human search for family love. The second part of this search involves building family relationships through which our need for love can be met. At this point in your courtship, how are the two of you doing at building family (in-law) relationships?

12. You are starting a new family, which will be separate (distinct, not necessarily geographically distant) from your two families of origin. How are you doing as a couple in establishing emotional distance from your families of origin? How are you doing as individuals at this task?

13. Society needs as many of its citizens as possible to become couples by successfully courting and marrying each other and going on from there to form strong and loving families. How have you experienced social support during your courtship? How have you experienced interference?

14. Courtship is a difficult and highly emotional time. It can be both exhilarating and defeating, empowering and heart breaking. What has been difficult about your courtship? What has been the best part?

Lesson Two

Personal Letter to Couples

Dear Precious Couples,

Welcome again. You may be reading this letter as part of your preparation for your second meeting with your pastor or Christian Educator or in preparation for a longer first meeting. In this letter, you and I are going to talk about the themes that are part of the discussion sheet labeled Lesson Two.

I want to start this second discussion with the topic of singleness. It may seem overly obvious to say you've been single and are now choosing to be married. Both of you clearly know this. Your upcoming marriage isn't something you've fallen into by accident or without conscious effort. But I want you to realize getting married cannot be about fleeing singleness. Being single has a stigma attached to it in our society. For example, there can be social pressure in some churches, and in some families, for singles to get married so they can fit in. It can seem like there are social activities for couples and for children but none designed for adult singles. You may have noticed that outside of college, there are few places for adult singles to hang out and meet – besides clubs and bars. You could say this problem has given rise to an entire industry of dating services.

Our churches and our society can be especially unwelcoming to unmarried adults. And, although the church may be more accommodating to couples, God does not show special favor to people who are paired off. Being married is natural, but so is being unmarried. Singleness is not a curse to run from. Single people can and do live valuable lives; they make important contributions to their families, their churches,

33

their communities, and to the security of their nation. Single people can and do experience the full range of loving experiences. They give love and care to family members. They invest themselves in loving friendships, and in various ways, they give loving service to the needy in their communities.

Think about it. Everyone is born single. People who do not find a mate for themselves remain single. People who do not choose to marry remain single. Married people who divorce return to being single as do married people whose partners die. Many of us spend a good share of our lives being single. God loves people; not married people or single people. God loves people.

One of my strongest beliefs about marriage is that it is a laboratory for learning to love with a Christ-like love. I believe this. But there's no way that I can make the case, once you two are married, you will have a better chance of learning to love. Neither can I make the case that, as a married couple, you will have better access to God. The New Testament makes it clear God's purpose in the life of every Christian is to teach us Christ-like love. Whether you two get married or stay single, learning Christ-like love will remain God's plan for you. My conviction is that life is the ultimate laboratory for learning to love as Christ loves. Marriage is just one important subcategory of life. As such, marriage gives us the opportunity to love in the face of life's hardships and blessings. But, in the words of Jesus, hardship and blessing fall like rain on everyone (Matthew 5:45).

I cannot tell you, for example, married people have families while single people don't. Everyone has a family – although of different sizes. Married couples end up with at least two families – perhaps three, or even more families, if their marriage is a second or third. But everyone starts with some combination of mother and father, parent or guardian, brothers and sisters, cousins, aunts and uncles. Single adults still have a mixture of these family relationships. And both couples and singles who live away from personal family relationships make family for themselves from the people they meet and grow close to in their neighborhood and jobs. The dynamics are very similar, if not identical, within the family of a married couple and within the created family of single individuals.

We all know the joke that we cannot choose our family members. This bit of levity is an admission family members can drive us nuts. Intimate family relationships can break our hearts and infuriate us. Strained family relationships can make us want to yell. Families confront us with folks who are difficult to love, but so can life in general. Family can bless our lives with folks whose love nurtures us, but so can life in general. Married couples and single individuals alike can experience the blessings and struggles of love.

Of course, whether we are single or married, we do make choices about our family. And we create family for ourselves. When we first move away from home, we create family for ourselves among our new friends. Newly married couples make decisions about which singles and which couples they will include in their inner circle, whom they will treat like family. Churches are a common resource for Christians to use in finding and building family. For example, adult single Christians often network and build family like relationships with fellow church members, gathering together socially, cooking together, and helping each other. In addition, members of the LGBTQ community often seek each other out and embrace each other as family. Sometimes this is because the church ostracizes them instead of including them in church social circles. Sometimes the warm acceptance of the church community forms a welcome addition to the family-like LGBTQ community relationships.

The point is every person's life finds meaning and richness in different ways. Your life, if you stayed a single person, could still achieve meaning and richness. Marriage is a wonderful thing; but it doesn't magically guarantee greater meaning, fuller richness, or perfect bliss. Marriage doesn't even always guarantee an end to loneliness. Marriage offers the opportunity, as does single living, to turn to our lone-liness into an experience of being alone that is made full by ongoing feelings of loving connection to family, friends, colleagues, and espe-cially to God.

Marriage isn't finally about doing everything with your partner, to-gether and side by side. It's about doing your daily work and activities, often separately and apart, but doing them for each other; so, whether together or apart, everything you do is out of love and the feeling of unbroken connection. Then, when you come together at day's end, you can talk about what each other did while apart. Your partner's work activities might not normally interest you. But they become interesting when you realize this work is done out of love for you.

Whether you were to remain single or whether you follow through on your commitment to marry, it will require work to create an ongoing experience of emotional intimacy. It will require learning to lovingly share the gift of your daily story. And it will require learning to share both your heart's happy moments and your heart's hurting moments. Both joy and pain are intense feelings and can be hard to put into words. Marriage is a very concentrated opportunity to learn the hard work of sharing intense emotions at times you feel vulnerable.

I came into marriage believing my strong feelings deserved to be heard and understood. I felt emotionally entitled and often shared my feelings believing them to have an elevated importance. Sometimes I was angry when I felt I wasn't being understood. I tended to see my strong feelings as deserving emotional drama. My wife tends to prefer emotional calm. She doesn't like her emotional waters stirred up by choppy emotional waves. The more emotional drama I produced, the calmer and less responsive she became. As I wrote before, we fought our way through couple's therapy. It took us several years for us to learn how to fight towards emotional understanding instead of fight-ing each other. You can expect marriage to give you the opportunity to fight with another person, on the same side with them instead of against them, in the effort to build mutual emotional understanding.

One major factor that will enable you as a married couple to keep fighting to build emotional understanding is the confidence God has brought you two together. I was so confident God had planned to bring my wife and me together I didn't even ask her to marry me. I asked her when we should start planning our wedding. She has good-naturedly harassed me over the years for never having gotten "down on one knee" and giving her the "will you marry me" speech. I actually believed our marriage wasn't our choice; it was God's choice for us. My wife finally came to see our marriage as God's plan for us.

My challenge for you now is to look beyond the story of how you two fell in love. I challenge you to look for signs of God's hand behind the events that brought you into each other's lives. Start to make a new story for yourselves by asking new questions. What signs has God given that you are meant to be together? How might the significant little coincidences in your story have been arranged by God? How have you become confident God wants you to build a loving family? How have you seen God's humor in the way you found each other? Ask yourselves how it gives you confidence to see signs that God's hand has been active in your life as a couple.

Confidence in yourselves as a couple is especially important because marriage will give you a close-up chance to see each other's weaknesses and brokenness. Christians call our weakness and brokenness *sin*. Because Christians believe our sin is forgiven, we need not shrink from facing our sin out of guilt or shame. Instead, as a Christian couple, you will be free to recognize that sin permeates the world and all human relationships – including yours. This will mean you can accept your compromised ability as a couple to form loving relationships. Accepting the disabling impact of sin in your lives can help you face, without feeling guilt or shame, the brokenness within each other that will make love a lifetime, uphill struggle. A joyful struggle. But a struggle that asks you to be understanding and accepting of each other's weaknesses and failings.

I cannot say too strongly that the Christian doctrine of sin is not about fearing God or about laboring under the weight of guilt or shame. Theologically, the doctrine of sin calls us to realize we need God's mercy. The Good News of the gospel tells us we have God's mercy and can trust God's acceptance. Marriage challenges us to show this same mercy and acceptance to each other and to ourselves.

Life will certainly put you in the vice of money problems, job pressures, family arguments, and all kinds of worries. These difficulties will bring out both your strengths and weaknesses. You'll gain the chance to admire each other's strengths; as well as the chance to show patience, tolerance, understanding, and acceptance in the face of each other's weaknesses. Loving your marriage partner with a Christ-like love is all about learning to demonstrate patience, tolerance, under-standing, and acceptance. My own experience is that treating my wife with this kind of understanding and acceptance has a personal payoff: I become more understanding and accepting of myself.

Enjoying each other's strengths is a fun part of marriage. But learning to accept your partner's weaknesses, as well as your own, deepens your shared appreciation of the human experience. The more deeply you both get in touch with your humanness, the more comfortable you will become with admitting your weakness and need to each other. Marriage helps us face our need for each other, our need for God, and our need for community – friends, family, and church. It may feel counterintuitive, but the more you can face and admit your needs, the stronger you become as a person and the stronger your marriage will become.

I said in the last lesson something I'm sure you both know: early in your love relationship you tend to be more tuned into your love for each other than you are tuned into the other loves in your lives. Let me add you are more likely, here at the outset of your love, to also be more tuned into your need for each other. Over time, though, you will be lucky to learn how much you also need God in your lives.

God's forgiveness and acceptance can help you learn to be forgiving and accepting of each other; and God's Spirit can help strengthen your weaknesses. Facing your failings can motivate you to turn to God for strength. Knowing where you are lacking can also motivate you to develop a prayer life. Too often though, couples don't learn to find strength in prayer until after they add young children to their lives. Sometimes this is because we adults are more concerned for our children's spiritual welfare than our own. Sometimes having children in our lives severely stresses our emotional, mental, and physical resources. Let me suggest you've no reason to wait to turn to God for strength. I suggest getting married can be enough of a challenge to motivate you to develop an active prayer and spiritual life. In fact, getting involved in church together, where you can both nurture your relationship with God, can be a real asset to your marriage.

That is why a Christian Marriage is essentially a three-way commitment. It is a commitment between you and your partner. It a commitment between you as a couple and God. And it is a commitment between you as couple and the Christian church community. A civil marriage is a contract between you as a couple and the state in which you live. All of us are familiar with state marriage law. We know, for example, some states define marriage using community property laws. We know states' laws give rights to married couples which they don't give to domestic partnerships. We know some states allowed same-sex marriage prior to the US Supreme Court decision and others did not. Civil marriage is actually defined somewhat differently by each state.

But Christian Marriage is yet a different kind of contract. Christian Marriage begins by acknowledging the essential role God plays in our lives together. It starts with the promise you make to each other before God to love each other for a lifetime. And it only remains strong as both partners keep themselves open to receiving God's strength. A vigorous prayer life, worship life, and Scripture study are essential aids to a strong Christian Marriage. Each of these spiritual practices may play a different role in your lives during different stages of your marriage. But it is important to your marriage as a Christian to do whatever you can to keep a nurturing and growing relationship with God.

I suspect it is easier to understand that our marriages need God than it is to understand that our marriages need church fellowship. We know Christian Marriages take place in church in the presence of the Christian community. But what exactly is the connection between the church and Christian Marriage? Let me see if I can explain it.

Most of us realize we need friends. Certainly each of you has friends now, before you are married, and some of those dear people will remain your friends as you formally become a married couple. But after you are married, you'll want couple friends. Couples tend to hang out socially with other couples. If it hasn't become an issue yet, it will become important to you as a couple to develop couple friends. The church can be a big help in this process.

The question some of you will surely ask is, "Why would we trust the church to be a place to build friendships?" The church isn't always a nurturing place. Jesus told his followers they should be known by their love for each other (John 13:35). But not all of you who are reading this will have had positive or loving experience with the church. If you are gay, your memories of the church may include damnation and rejection. You may have been taught God hates you and the church has no place for you. It's entirely possible the church has loaded you down with the weight of guilt and shame that has plagued your life. It's possible you've been saddled with a belief in God mixed with a fear of God, neither of which you can escape.

There are corners of the Christian church which teach this kind of fearful faith to both straight and gay people. There are some places where the church has been an equal opportunity oppressor of its members. There are both gay and straight Christians who have been raised with hatred for their sexuality. Some of you may have experienced the church as a large, loving family. But some of you may have experienced the church as hostile and spiritually hurtful. As Christians, the church is our spiritual family whether that family is supportive or dysfunctional.

I'm suggesting that Christian married couples need the church in a way similar to their need for the support of their earthly extended family. In either case, that support might not be forthcoming. Our earthly family and the earthly church are both comprised of sinful humans. And both family and church will certainly fall short of being perfectly loving and understanding. Some of us will have abusive families, and many of us will have a strange or hostile relative or two. Some of us have had spiritually abusive relationships with the church. But I want you to know, as a Christian married couple, the Christian church should be giving you certain essential kinds of support.

In Ephesians chapter five, where Paul defines Christian Marriage, he bases his admonition that couples are one and equal, and need to love each other with a Christ-like love, on the premise that couples are "members of his body" (Ephesians 5:30). Not only are individual Christians members of Christ's body (I Corinthians 6:15), but Christian couples are also jointly members of that body. Not only do individual Christians need the support and ministry of fellow Christians (Ephesians 4:12-13), but so do married Christian couples.

I'm suggesting Christian couples can contribute something essential to your marriage relationship that you won't get from couples who don't share your Christian faith. Perhaps it is an intangible something. But to paraphrase the words of Ephesians chapter four, Christian couples can edify us, complete us as people, strengthen us, and energize our faith. What you can gain from the Christian couples you meet, only you can discover. But the point is churches owe a ministry of hospitality to their couple members, and you should expect to be included in the couples' fellowship of the church you belong to. It will also mean that as couple members of your church, you will need to show hospitality to other couples.

41

Here's what this means for you. As you consider Christian Marriage, look for a church with friendly couples whom you can get to know. The skill of hospitality will help you develop these contacts into friendships. Whether your church calls the Lord's Supper "Communion" or "Eucharist," every Christian is welcome at the table of our Lord. One of the things this means is no church member is to be denied Christian fellowship; so expect to be included in the church community. I suggest you, as a couple, make a point of affiliating with church that both welcomes you at the Lord's Supper, and welcomes you into its fellowship.

At the church you as a couple choose to attend, you will want to develop a supportive network of Christian friends. This will mean learning to ask for and accepting help from the families in the church community and cultivating the grace of hospitality towards them. Christian Marriage invites you to accept your weaknesses and needs and to look to each other, to God, and to the Christian community for strength. And it means expecting to find that strength from all three sources.

Warmly in Christ,

Steve

The Rev. Steve R. Wigall, Th.M., Th.D.

Lawrence, Massachusetts

How irreverent are the stiff and stuffy!
Who is less Godly than those who reject joy and laughter?
Who dishonors the Creator more than those who refuse to be earthy?
How wild and beautiful our God – who is in love with all creation
and every person!
Who can keep God's love from healing human hearts with celestial
laughter and joy?

LESSON TWO

DISCUSSION QUESTIONS

Class Opening

> (Leader) Gracious God, (pray in unison) **teach us to love each other as a couple with a Christ-like love. Teach us to know each other as Christ knows us. Teach us to take joy in each other as Christ takes joy in us.**
>
> **When love gets hard, let us be patient with each other as you are patient. Let us strive to be understanding as you understand. Let us be faithful to each other as you are faithful.**
>
> **Grant that, through our shared successes and failures, through our shared happiness and sorrow, we might find lasting joy in the lessons of love which you teach us. We pray in the name of Jesus Christ, who shows us your love, calls us to love, and empowers us with your love. Amen**

Christian Marriage *Is All About* **. . . Learning to Love**

The Discipline of Family Love **is both joyous and vexing because it involves us in relationships that confront us with life's greatest blessings and life's greatest difficulties. God intends for us to grow in our ability to love through being enriched by the blessings of family love and strengthened by its difficulties.**

Questions to discuss:

1. What questions do you have from the Couple's Pamphlet or from the Couple's Letter(s)? Ask the couple or couples, "Is there homework from our last session? Are there questions that have come to your mind since we last met or talked?" Share homework.

2. To what degree are you getting married because of the pressure of family and friends? Has that pressure been a helpful motivator or an unhelpful interference?

3. Would adult, single Christians be right to feel deprived or feel like social outsiders? If you do not get married, or if your marriage partner dies, would you face the end of a valuable life or an end to experiencing love? Why or why not?

4. Do you believe singleness is a status God honors and blesses? How can the meaning and the richness of love can be experienced by unmarried persons?

5. Would it change your life to believe coital sex belongs exclusively in faithful marriage relationships? If so, how?

Starting a new family by marrying a life partner is not the only way to learn the lessons of love. Singleness is also a normal part of human life. All married people begin life by being single and may become single again if their marriage ends. Many people are single for a lifetime. Fortunately, God can bring all the blessing and discipline of love into the lives of people who find themselves single, or who choose to remain single.

Questions to discuss:

6. Seeking Christian Marriage is seeking a good thing. Can you see signs God has led you to want to create a family of your own? Can you see signs God has led you to find that special marriage partner with whom to create it? What signs have you seen?

7. Approach Christian Marriage with every hope of happiness and joy; but realize, even with God's blessing, your marriage will not achieve unbroken bliss. What skills do you bring to your marriage for coping with its inevitable disappointments?

8. Couples seeking Christian Marriage need to be realistic about how difficult it will be to keep growing for a lifetime in the love for their chosen partner. What strategies do you bring to your marriage for keeping love alive?

9. Take stock, as best you can, of your readiness to meet the demands of love throughout all of life's stages and crises. As Jesus said, a builder will take stock of his supplies before he begins to build a tower; and, before a king goes to war, he will count the size of his army and the sufficiency of his ammunition.

> **For which of you, desiring to build a tower, does not first sit down and count the cost, whether he has enough to complete it? Otherwise, when he has laid a foundation and is not able to finish, all who see it begin to mock him, saying, 'This man began to build and was not able to finish.' Or what king, going out to encounter another king in war, will not sit down first and deliberate whether he is able with ten thousand to meet him who comes against him with twenty thousand? And if not, while the other is yet a great way off, he sends a delegation and asks for terms of peace. So therefore, any one of you who does not renounce all that he has cannot be my disciple. (Luke 14:28–33).**

Homework: To facilitate taking stock, make a list of the 3 to 5 hardest challenges you anticipate facing together in your married life. Share and discuss each other's lists. Decide and mark how tough each life challenge might be on a scale of 1 to 10, with 1 being easiest and 10 being hardest.

However, God *commonly* brings the discipline of love into human life through marriage and family. God even encourages people to look for a life partner whom they can marry and work with to create a new family. Christian Marriage is a good thing; but it offers neither a magic ticket to human happiness nor guarantees the new family a couple creates will be perfectly loving.

Questions to discuss:

10. The love that brings two people together in marriage is strong and creates the feeling within the couple, together, they can do anything. What experiences have you had that shake your confidence in each other? At this point in time, how would you describe the strengths you see in your partner that give you confidence in him or her?

11. At the outset of marriage, it is important for Christian couples to recognize, because of their human weakness and brokenness, they will need God to be a third partner in their marriage. What signs have you seen you need God in your relationship?

12. How have you included God in your courtship? What specific activities can you as a couple do to make God an active part of your marriage?

Christians believe sin permeates the world and damages the human ability to form relationships – including family relationships. Consequently, accepting Christian Marriage means accepting learning *The Discipline of Family Love* will be an ongoing and sometimes uphill, lifetime struggle.

Questions to discuss:

13. When you look back at the marriage, or lack of marriage, of your childhood caregiver(s) and your early family life, you will see imperfections and even failures. What aspects of these marriages and formative families do you admire?

14. Accepting the failures in our family of origin can make it easier to accept our own failures to love perfectly. What 2 or 3 aspects of your family of origin do you have trouble accepting?

Christian Marriage *Is All About* . . . Living in Community.

The presence of sin in the world means no one comes to Christian Marriage with a perfect experience of family love. It also means married couples can expect creating a loving family will require a lifetime of work.

Consequently, every Christian family needs the support of the Christian faith community to help it handle *The Discipline of Family Love*. As all Christian people are welcome at Christ's communion table and none are to be excluded; so all Christian families are welcome in the supportive communion of Christ's church, and none are to be excluded.

When we accept Christian Marriage and become a Christian family, we will be called to reach out to and support the other families in the church community. In return, we should expect the welcome of church families and be prepared to receive their support.

Questions to discuss:

15. To meet the challenges of family love, a Christian couple will need the strength and support of their church family. What hesitations do you have about asking for and accepting help from the church community?

16. A healthy marriage cannot exist in isolation. What might be hard about cultivating and accepting the friendship and encouragement of other loving Christian families?

17. The commitment of Christian Marriage is not only between (1) the two of you. It is also between (2) yourselves and God, and between (3) yourselves and the church community. How do you feel about entering into a "three way" marriage commitment?

18. What strategies might you use for developing the kind of trusting relationships with other Christian couples that would allow for mutual support? What kind of activities do you think help create trust between couples?

19. Building a supportive network for your marriage will involve cultivating the grace of hospitality. How do you feel about using your home to extend friendship, table fellowship when possible, and help when needed, to other Christian couples within your faith community? Are you more temperamentally inclined to want your home to be an emotional refuge or to be a social center? How would each of you balance these two goals? (It is likely each of you will prefer a different balance.)

LESSON THREE

PERSONAL LETTER TO COUPLES

Dear Precious Couples,

Welcome again. In this lesson, we'll continue discussing *The Discipline of Family Love*. That is what I'm calling the guidance Scripture gives Christian married couples. Let me point out something you may already realize: Marriage guidance is not located in one particular section of Scripture. We find guidance for married couples in the Old Testament Torah, specifically in The Ten Commandments. We also find marriage guidance in Old Testament wisdom literature, specifically the Song of Solomon. And we'll look at several New Testament epistles, particularly, in the epistles of Paul. There we'll find significant marriage guidance offered in the context of his discussion of the relationship between Christ and the church.

One at a time, we'll discuss key scriptural passages that give marriage guidance. For the purposes of these letters, I'll take off my formal teaching hat, and just talk with you about these verses, as though we were sitting at a lunch table talking informally. I expect you'll have the chance to discuss the verses in more detail with your pastor or counselor.

"You shall not commit adultery." (Exodus 20:14)

When you look to Scripture for marriage guidance, you'll find two primary moral instructions. Both were given to Moses by God in the context of the Ten Commandments. You might think from listening to some Christian preachers that God gives different moral guidance to his straight children from the guidance he gives to his gay children. But not so. God's moral instructions are the same for all couples – gay or straight. The first moral instruction is: Don't commit adultery.

This means: be faithful to the one you love. Do not betray the one you love by being sexually unfaithful to them. Interestingly, the Ten Commandments do not specifically define marriage. But in the context of Scripture as a whole, we can accept this verse as Scripture's marriage definition. We can understand marriage as a commitment between two people, before God, to be sexually faithful to each other. The Christian meaning of this commandment, then, is that Christian Marriage takes place when a couple commits before God, and the Christian community, to enter a lifelong sexually faithful relationship.

Christians value marriage highly. In Catholic tradition, marriage is even considered a sacrament. Among Protestant churches, marriage is considered a sacred commitment. In this light, it is surprising how little Scripture says about marriage. Many marriage traditions are mentioned in Scripture: betrothal, wedding feasts, and grooms paying for brides. But marriage is nowhere defined in Scripture – except in Exodus 20:14. The verse doesn't say, "This is the meaning of marriage." But this verse is the only command among the Ten that describes the covenant of sexual faithfulness, the covenant that comprises marriage.

Perhaps because adultery is usually understood as a prohibition against sexual unfaithfulness by married individuals, I've heard it suggested this verse doesn't apply to people who aren't married. There's a common belief, even among some Christians, that Christian morality requires something like serial monogamy. The idea is, that before marriage, active sexual relationships are ok . . . as long as we are sexually involved with only one person at a time. Then, after marriage, there's no more "messing around." A lifetime commitment to being sexually faithful to just one person, in this view, is only required of married couples. I suggest that's not what the verse says. I suggest the verse describes a whole-life sexual lifestyle of faithfulness to one person.

It's not surprising Scripture defines marriage in terms of faithfulness. One of the primary ways God is described is as faithful. (E.g. Deuteronomy 7:9; Isaiah 47:9; 11 Timothy 2:13). In Ephesians 5:32,

Paul describes married love as God-like, or, more specifically as Christ-like. Married love is self-sacrificial, like Christ's love, in that it gives itself for the one it loves. It is like God's love in that it is faithful.

We'll go into this more in a later lesson. But Scripture doesn't separate sexual intercourse from marriage. In a very real sense, sex before marriage isn't possible. Sexual intercourse constitutes marriage. The serial monogamy many people practice actually amounts to their involvement in multiple informal marriages, going from one to the next, without the benefit of divorce. People who are involved with a series of sexual partners before marriage may not have legally divorced before they moved on. But I suggest they have experienced the moral and spiritual equivalent of divorce.

The idea of moral divorce is not commonly discussed. I bring it up here as a way to think about the reality of the bond between two people created by sexual intercourse and the reality of the rupture caused by ending that relationship. Legally constituted divorce is usually considered a sin. Jesus said divorce was not in God's original plan for humanity (Matthew 19:8). I suggest, for our purposes, we can understand moral or spiritual divorce to be a sin in the sense it causes moral or spiritual damage. Sexual intercourse constitutes the moral and spiritual bond of marriage. Breaking that bond, by ending that relationship, to a greater or lesser degree, creates the moral and spiritual damage of a divorce.

I expect that many of you who are reading this book, and who are planning to get married, have been involved in prior sexual relationships. Some of you may have been legally married and legally divorced. But some of you have been sexually involved and then terminated that relationship without the benefit of legal marriage or legal divorce. I'm suggesting, on the basis of Exodus 20:14, you've been though the moral and spiritual equivalent of marriage and divorce. So, what is the significance of this?

The point isn't to find something else to feel guilty about or be ashamed of. Since we're starting this discussion with the Ten Commandments we need to talk about what the commandments mean to teach us. What are we supposed to realize from acknowledging that the command-ments have pinpointed our sin? Let me be clear. We don't face our sins in order to pile on the guilt and shame. We face the sin in our lives to realize the ways life has hurt and damaged us and created our need for mercy. We learn we need God's mercy. We need our own mercy. And we need our partner's mercy.

We have God's mercy; we just need to accept it. But too many of us struggle to give ourselves the mercy, understanding, and acceptance we need. Paul explains we all need mercy, because none of us keep the commandments. Romans 3:23, "All of us fall short of the glory of God's standards." Romans 3:10, "No one is righteous." Romans 3:12, "No one does good." To convince us we cannot keep God's command-ments, Jesus explains God isn't just looking for good behaviors; God also judges our attitudes. For example, in Matthew 5:27-28, Jesus de-fines adultery as, not just the action of sexual unfaithfulness, but also having the thought of using someone for our sexual pleasure – an atti-tude common to human experience. Jesus makes the point that we cannot pretend we've achieved goodness just because we've not done anything especially bad, because God also looks at our attitudes, which give away the sin that works within our minds and emotions (Matthew 15:19-20). The point is we've all experienced damage from the sin in our lives; we all need mercy.

Here's how this relates to married life. None of us comes into marriage unscathed. None of us come into marriage able to claim a position of moral superiority. All of us enter marriage as broken people wounded by sin in different ways. That wounding may or may not include prior sexual relationships. But all of us enter marriage wounded in our abili-ty to love. And in relationship to the command to not commit adultery, yes, God is telling us all to avoid being sexually unfaithful. Don't do it. It causes major hurt and pain. But be merciful to yourself and your partner. Be understanding. Over the long haul of marriage, expect to run into various kinds of betrayals and unfaithfulness. Work hard to prevent sexual betrayal, and work hard to prevent intentional betrayals of all kinds. But accept that unintentional and accidental betrayals will occur. You both will need each other's mercy.

You shall not lust after your neighbor's house; you shall not lust after your neighbor's wife, or his male servant, or his female servant, or his ox, or his donkey, or anything that is your neighbor's. (Exodus 20:17)

The second moral instruction for married couples also comes from the Ten Commandments, Exodus 20:17. In our discussion of the com-mandment against adultery, we saw that Jesus referred to the commandments against adultery and lust as a part of the same command. He said, "everyone who looks at a woman with lust has already committed adultery with her in his heart." But to be fair, we should note the command against lust, as expressed in Exodus, seems morally questionable to modern people. Listed among our neighbor's possessions, for which we must not lust, are his wife, his house, his male servant, and his female servant. It doesn't make us feel better to say that in the culture of Exodus, wives and servants could be considered as possessions, like animals and houses. We're not willing anymore to accept the idea a human being can be anyone's property.

So, as we talk about lust, I'll try to interpret it the same way Jesus seemed to have. Jesus seemed to treat the ownership of human beings as a kind of red herring. He doesn't comment on it as a legal matter. Instead, he focuses on lust as a destructive attitude. His emphasis is on the problem of treating either a woman or a man as a possession which can be owned, and especially on the problem of treating a human be-ing as a sexual object which can be used as a tool for our gratification. You can own a house or ox or donkey. You may do what pleases you with your house or ox or donkey. But a man or woman cannot be your possession and must not be treated as one. We must not treat each oth-er as something we can use to gratify us sexually.

If I were to put this commandment in modern terms for Christian mar-ried couples, I'd say it this way. Do not lust after the one you love. And this means: Do not violate the one you love by sexually objectifying or using them. A question which will further clarify the meaning of lust might be, "What is the difference between sexually enjoying each other and using someone as a tool of sexual gratification?" It is important to point out the difference isn't between acceptable sexual activities and unacceptable ones. Whatever two people enjoy, and harms neither one, is morally acceptable. The moral difference rests in our attitude towards each other.

I suggest the attitude of lust can be best understood by looking at the story of King David and Bathsheba (II Samuel 11:2-4). Let me quickly summarize the story. David sees Bathsheba bathing on her rooftop. He becomes sexually excited. So far, this is not lust. Sexual feelings are not lust and are not sin. But then David decides he wants to possess Bathsheba. This is lust. He is king and can get what he wants. He sends his men to fetch her. She comes to the palace. He has sex with her. He sends her home. David wanted her. He took her. He used her for his sexual pleasure. When he was done with her, he sent her back. This is lust, in both attitude and action. Lust is the desire to possess and use another person for our sexual gratification. And it dehumanizes us when we give in to it.

> **Do you not know that your bodies are members of Christ? Shall I then take the members of Christ and make them members of a prostitute? Never! Or do you not know that he who is joined to a prostitute becomes one body with her? For, as it is written, "The two will become one flesh." But he who is joined to the Lord becomes one spirit with him. Flee from sexual immorality. Every other sin a person commits is outside the body, but the sexually immoral person sins against his own body. Or do you not know that your body is a temple of the Holy Spirit within you, whom you have from God? You are not your own, for you were bought with a price. So glorify God in your body. (1 Corinthians 6:15-20)**

These verses essentially make one point. Our bodies are sacred to God. The word "sacred" does not appear in this text; but the point is made. Sacred means: set apart for the service of God. Our bodies "are members of Christ," "joined to the Lord," and are "one spirit with him." Our bodies belong to Christ who bought us, and are set apart for God's service, as "temples of the Holy Spirit" who lives within us. It's interesting that Paul, who was a Pharisee by training, doesn't argue against sexual immorality, in this case with a prostitute, by appealing to the Ten Commandments. Instead, he argues we should be motivated to avoid sexual immorality by realizing our bodies are sacred to God who owns us, is one with us, and dwells within us.

This is an important sexual principle for Christian couples. Paul suggests one of the strongest motivations we as couples can have to avoid sexually immorality is our recognition that both of us are sacred to God. Our goal as Christians must be to learn to treat the bodies of our loved ones as sacred. This process starts for us when we realize all people are sacred to God. It reaches completion for couples when we learn to treat ourselves and each other as sacred. For us as Christian couples, then, the profound knowledge that our bodies are sacred to God powerfully motivates us neither to sexually violate nor betray ourselves or each other.

> **Submit to one another out of reverence for Christ. Wives and Husbands Wives, submit to your own husbands, as to the Lord. For the husband is the head of the wife even as Christ is the head of the church, his body, and is himself its Savior. Now as the church submits to Christ, so also wives should submit in everything to their husbands. Husbands, love your wives, as Christ loved the church and gave himself up for her, that he might sanctify her, having cleansed her by the washing of water with the word, so that he might present the church to himself in splendor, without spot or wrinkle or any such thing, that she might be holy and without blemish. This mystery is profound, and I am saying that it refers to Christ and the church. (Ephesians 5:21 – 27, 32)**

55

This passage is usually studied and discussed for its teaching that Christian Marriage partners are called to love each other with a Christ-like love. But, I want to point out another point this passage makes. The bulk of this passage is a description of Christ's self-sacrificial love. Christ loved his church, of which we are spiritual members as people of God; and gave himself for us to cleanse us and present us to himself in splendor, making us holy and without blemish.

Loving each other with a Christ-like love doesn't save or make us holy. The passage isn't finally about the love between married people. The passage focuses on the love between "Christ and the church." The point is, Christian married couples are saved and made holy because they are individually members of the church whom Christ loves. Our efforts to love each other with a Christ-like love do not save and cleanse us. As hard as we try, our love for each other will fall short of being as self-sacrificial as Christ's love for us. Christian married couples are saved and loved, cleansed and holy, because Christ loves us individually as members of his church. A Christian couple who loves each other with a faithful, Christ-like love is "without spot or wrinkle or blemish" because they are both loved as part of Christ's body.

> **Let marriage be held in honor among all, and let the marriage bed be undefiled, for God will judge the sexually immoral and adulterous. (Hebrews 13:4)**

This verse in Hebrews, although it is not directly connected to Ephesians chapter five, expands on the same idea. It describes the conditions under which married couples have Christ's blessing. The Ephesians passage says married couples have Christ's spiritual blessings when they are both members of Christ's church. Hebrews says the sexual relationship which married couples enjoy has Christ's blessing when both partners are sexually faithful to each other. To say it another way, when married couples love each other as does God – with a faithful love (like Christ's love for the church), their sexual relationship is honored and blessed by God.

God wants to free married couples from any idea their sex lives are evil, or dirty, or anything but God-blessed. But, contrary to a good deal of propaganda spread by some churches, God's blessing on marriage has nothing to do with the supposed requirement that Christian Marriage should consist of "one man and one woman." This phrase appears nowhere in Scripture. And, unfortunately, it has functioned to distract the church's attention from the one scriptural requirement for God's blessing on a marriage: sexual faithfulness.

> **Oh that you were like a brother to me, who nursed at my mother's breasts! If I found you outside, I would kiss you, and none would despise me. (Song of Solomon 8:1)**

This is a wonderful passage. The speaker in Song of Solomon chapter 8, is the bride who describes herself as "the Rose of Sharon" (2:1). She is speaking about her groom whom she calls her Beloved. She describes their ideal romantic relationship as being open and unashamed as though between a brother and sister. The point is not that romantic love is brotherly or sisterly. The point is, healthy, vibrant romantic love is naturally unafraid to openly demonstrate its loving feelings and its affection.

Healthy romantic love has no desire to sneak around and conceal itself. When the love between two people is strong and vital, they neither desire to hide their love from family and friends, nor want to withdraw from social activities. A strong and vital romantic love is proud to be openly affectionate, especially in front of loved ones. This love is not burdened by either shame or guilt. Nor does it struggle with a desire for secrecy. Ask yourselves as a couple: Have you ever been tempted to sneak behind the backs of, or hide your romantic relationship from, family and friends? Or, is there a set of relatives or friends around whom you don't feel free to express your affection? If so, you may want to consider this a warning sign. A couple whose love is strong is proud of their feelings of love, and unashamed to express them – wherever *it is safe* for them to do so.

The open and unashamed display of your couple affection is an ideal. Straight couples may notice family, and even people in general, especially older couples, smile at them when they hold hands or kiss in public. Gay couples may have a very different experience. When they hold hands or kiss in public, they may have more likely received stares or frowns, or even been subject to open hostility. This kind of negativity may come from older couples and even couples from their own family.

Public Display of Affection (PDA) can be a tricky thing to navigate. My personal observation, I smile happily as I write this, is when we are younger, we more often misjudge how much PDA is acceptable in a particular social context. Younger couples sometimes can't seem to keep their hands off of each other. But those young days are good times. And older couples are often tolerant of the affectionate enthusiasm of the young. As young people gain experience, they learn to judge how much PDA is going to be accepted.

The unfortunate truth is gay couples often do not receive the same encouragement as straight couples. This is really tragic. As a society, we need to encourage young love, and to cheer on courting couples. If any change needs to take place with the increasing social acceptance of Marriage Equality, it is the open encouragement of gay couples who are courting. Couples who have to sneak around and hide their affection for each other have a harder time entering into and establishing strong and lasting marriages.

Warmly in Christ,

Steve

The Rev. Steve R. Wigall, Th.M., Th.D.

Lawrence, Massachusetts

How irreverent are the stiff and stuffy!
Who is less Godly than those who reject joy and laughter?
Who dishonors the Creator more than those who refuse to be earthy?
How wild and beautiful our God – who is in love with all creation
and every person!
Who can keep God's love from healing human hearts with celestial
laughter and joy?

LESSON THREE

DISCUSSION QUESTIONS

Class Opening

(Leader) Gracious God, (pray in unison) **teach us to love each other as a couple with a Christ-like love. Teach us to know each other as Christ knows us. Teach us to take joy in each other as Christ takes joy in us.**

When love gets hard, let us be patient with each other as you are patient. Let us strive to be understanding as you understand. Let us be faithful to each other as you are faithful.

Grant that through our shared successes and failures, through our shared happiness and sorrow, we might find lasting joy in the lessons of love which you teach us. We pray in the name of Jesus Christ, who shows us your love, calls us to love, and empowers us with your love. Amen

The Discipline of Family Love: I - V

Clearly, Christian Marriage is *so much more* **than a relationship between two people who love each other and want to spend their lives together. But, what exactly does the** *so much more* **of Christian Marriage ask couples to** *do***?**

Christian Marriage asks couples to accept *The Discipline of Family Love***. For couples, this means taking the following actions, and living by the following values, all of which find their basis in the teaching of Scripture.**

I.   Be faithful to the one you love.

Do not betray the one you love by being sexually unfaithful to them.

(Exodus 20:14)

Questions to discuss:

1. What questions do you have from the Couple's Pamphlet or from the Couple's Letter(s)? Ask the couple or couples, "Is there homework from our last session? Are there questions that have come to your mind since we last met or talked?" Share homework.

2. Exodus 20:14 (above), is the first and most important moral commandment that applies to marriage. How does American culture help strengthen marriage and make faithfulness easier? How does American culture undermine marriage and make faithfulness harder?

3. The *Christian* meaning of this commandment is marriage requires a couple to commit before God and the Christian community to enter a lifelong sexually faithful relationship. How do you feel about the essential moral foundation of marriage being sexual faithfulness? Is this too strict a standard? Why or why not?

4. Do not "lust after" the one you love.

    a. This means: do not violate the one you love by sexually objectifying or using them.

    b. (Matthew 5:28; James 1:14; Exodus 20:17)

Exodus 20:17 (above), is the second moral commandment that applies to marriage. The desire (lust or covetousness) being forbidden isn't sexual desire; sexual desire is a natural part of human life. The lust that is forbidden is described by Exodus 20:17 as first seeing a woman, like your neighbor's wife, as though she were in the same category as any other *thing* your neighbor *owns*. The sexual lust that is forbidden then desires to take that woman and use her for personal gratification as though she were a just a possession, or as we might say in contemporary language, to use her as a sexual object. Neither a woman nor a man is a possession which can be owned, or a sexual object which can be used as a tool for gratification.

> 5. What is the difference between sexually gratifying each other and using each other as a tool of gratification?

A woman is not a house, or ox, or donkey, or even a servant. Both a woman and a man are persons whose rights must be honored, human beings who deserve to be sexually treasured.

> 6. What might it mean to sexually treasure your marriage partner?

Perhaps the quintessential example of sexual lust is the story of David and Bathsheba (II Samuel 12:1–5). David is a king, and a powerful man capable of making things happen. From the high roof of his Jerusalem house, he looks out and sees a beautiful woman bathing on the roof of her home. This woman is Bathsheba. David is consumed with the desire to sexually possess Bathsheba. He doesn't care about what she wants or about the impact of his behavior on her life. David has her brought to his bed, has sex with her, and then sends her home. David neither sees nor treats Bathsheba as a person with rights to be honored. He uses her sexually and sends her away.

> 7. How do you judge David's behavior towards Bathsheba?

2. Treat the one you love as sacred.

When we realize that people are sacred to God, we learn to treat ourselves and each other as sacred. That is why we neither sexually violate nor betray ourselves or each other.

(1 Corinthians 6:13–20)

<u>Questions to discuss</u>:

> 8. Sacred (or holy) means, belonging to God and set aside for God's purposes. Your body is sacred (holy) to God; and your partner's body is sacred (holy) to God. What are some ways a couple might treat each other that shows they *do* hold each other as physically and sexually sacred?

> 9. The reason we don't sexually violate ourselves or our partner is we recognize both of us are sacred to God. We don't sexually betray ourselves or our partner for the same reason. What are some ways couples treat each other that might show they *do not* hold each other as physically and sexually sacred?

3. Realize that married sex is God-blessed.

All human relationships are infected by sin, including every human sexual relationship. The Good News is that when married couples love each other as does God – with a faithful love (like Christ's love for the church), their sexual relationship has God's blessing. God wants to free married couples from any idea that their sex lives are evil, or dirty, or anything but God-blessed.

(Romans 3:10 – 18, Ephesians 5:21 – 33, Hebrews 13:4)

<u>Questions to discuss</u>:

> 10. Is there ever any reason for a Christian couple to think their sexual relationship is evil, or dirty, or anything but God-blessed? Why or why not?

> 11. The faithful sexual relationship of Christian couple is blessed by God. Does sexual unfaithfulness revoke God's blessing on a Christian couple's sexual relationship? Why or why not?

12. If there is sexual unfaithfulness in a marriage, what can allow a fresh beginning, forgiveness, healing, and cleansing? Have you (for any reason) had to go through an experience of betrayal and reconciliation while dating? How did you handle the experience?

13. How does it feel to imagine your Christian Marriage will only last a lifetime if neither of you makes big mistakes? How does it feel to imagine you will make many marriage mistakes which will require you as a couple to stop and renegotiate your marriage to meet changing feelings, needs and desires? Do you envision your marriage as the successful run of a life-long marathon, or, as the successful run of many sprints, with numerous stops and numerous new beginnings? Which vision is more realistic? Which would be easier?

14. Being pushed to anger is not a threat to emotional well being; it is a normal part of the course of love. But can forgiveness ever be appropriate when there has been a realistic threat to your physical health or emotional well being? Why or why not?

4.   **Be unashamed of your loving feelings and affection.**

When the love between two people is vibrant and healthy, they neither desire to hide their love from friends, nor want to withdraw themselves from society – either out of shame or guilt or out of a desire for secrecy. They are proud and unashamed to express their feelings of love.

(Song of Solomon 8:1)

Questions to discuss:

15. A healthy romantic love is proud to be openly affectionate in front of loved ones. Have you ever been tempted to sneak behind the backs of, or hide your romantic relationship from

family and friends? Is there a set of relatives or friends around whom you don't feel free to express your affection? Why do you think this might be?

16. Respond to this statement. If you feel guilty before your family about being with the one you love, or feel the need to keep your romantic relationship secret, think carefully before deciding to marry him or her.

LESSON FOUR

PERSONAL LETTER TO COUPLES

Dear Precious Couples,

Welcome back to our discussion of *The Discipline of Family Love*, the guidance that Scripture gives to married Christian couples. We'll continue looking at the important scriptural passages that offer us direction for building a strong and loving marriage. Let's dive right in.

> **I would lead you and bring you into the house of my mother — she who used to teach me. (Song of Solomon 8:2)**

The first two verses of Song of Solomon, chapter eight, give us valuable insights into married life. Last lesson we looked at verse one: "Oh that you were like a brother to me, who nursed at my mother's breasts! If I found you outside, I would kiss you, and none would despise me." Verse one makes the point a strong and vibrant married love doesn't desire to hide itself away in secrecy. It embraces its opportunities to openly share with the whole world, and especially with family and friends, the warmth of its loving affection.

In this lesson, we're looking at what verse two says about the essential "family" part of family love. Married love is not just a private matter between two people. Married love has the desire to include its partner in the family where it grew up. So the love you two share as a couple has the ability to expand the family ties of the families in which you were raised. Your couple love has the ability to include new people into your childhood family: your partner and any children you two have or adopt.

Notice in this verse, that the bride in Song of Solomon, the Rose of Sharon, expresses her desire to bring her Beloved groom to her mother's house. She wants him to be a part of her family. This desire is a natural and healthy part of married love. The injunction Scripture gives you as a couple is to share your lives and your love with your extended families. Yes, marriage is about starting a new family. There is the element in marriage that involves leaving your father and mother (Ephesians 5:31) and establishing a life independent from your parents. But it is also true that newly married couples need to find a way to embrace each other's family (i.e. to take each other home to their parents.)

Ah, families. They can be wonderful and horrible. They can be a source of life-giving support and maddening challenges. Gay couples may even have to deal with one or both sets of in-laws who openly reject their marriage. The marriage of their gay or lesbian child may cause some parents to turn cold and hostile towards their child and his or her loving partner. This coldness and rejection is a tragedy and a loss for both parents and children.

But to be honest, gay couples are not the only victims of parental rejection. The Rose of Sharon in The Song of Solomon may have had reason to gladly welcome her groom into her mother's family. But not all of us were issued warm and welcoming families. Not all of us come to adulthood with close and intimate relationships with our parents. We finally must deal with the parents we have, whether cold or loving, not the ones we might wish for.

It is important to note that Song of Solomon 8:2 contains a strong implied injunction for parents. Parents are to raise their children with the promise that they can welcome and include their marriage partner in the family. You might say parents have an implied contract with their children. When your children are born, you as parents welcome them as family members with full rights. As parents, you take on the responsibility to give your children all the love and nurture and physical support you can. But a parent's promise to their children doesn't stop when childhood ends.

67

By making a child a full family member, you give him or her the unwritten but unquestionable right to include into full family membership the life partner they choose to love. Not all parents live up to this promise. But clearly, as parents, you will need to find a way to embrace your children's married family: their spouse and their children. Scripture describes married love as embracing multiple generations. That married love, into which you couples are entering, calls you to embrace your partner, the children you may have together, and the family your children will create should they get married. It is the essential nature of God's covenant love that it extends a "steadfast love to . . . those who love me . . . even to the third and fourth generation" (Exodus 20:6, paraphrased). Christian married love similarly reaches out to embrace those of its family members belonging to multiple generations.

Of course, in reality, there may be physical or emotional distance between you as a couple and your in-laws. Your parents or your in-laws might not open their hearts to fully welcome your family into their own. Life and work commitments may require you to live in a distant state from which traveling to be with your in-laws is very difficult. Perhaps at times, traveling to be with your in-laws and extended family may be too costly. We have to live with the situations we really face, not with situations we'd like, or with those Scripture describes as ideal.

Suppose you face one or both sets of in-laws who do not welcome your marriage. My prayer for you is that you don't have to face such a tragic situation. But let's be honest; couples do have to sometimes deal with such sad circumstances. I suggest, if you face unwelcoming in-laws, God would want you to be patient and forgiving. Forgive their coldness and patiently keep on hoping their attitudes might change. But be realistic. Adjust your expectations for unwelcoming family members and protect yourselves from the damaging impact of their rejection. If your parents or in-laws resist including you in their family, and resist being included in your family. it makes perfect sense to stop expecting their loving welcome.

Let me suggest, in this kind of hostile family situation, you would do well to give up your expectations. You would be wise to politely avoid contact with rejecting family members. When social contact is necessary continue to be polite for your own sake. But even as you learn to give up expecting hostile family members to welcome you, you may still hope against hope.

People can change and prayer can work miracles. I suggest you protect your emotions by not expecting a miracle to transform your rejecting family members into warm and cuddly teddy bears. But you can still pray for them, and can still hope for the miracle, however unlikely.

Your wife will be like a fruitful vine within your house; your children will be like olive shoots around your table. (Psalm 128:3)

Married love is essentially nurturing and creative. This verse from Psalms expresses the essential creative and fertile nature of a married couple's love. It is important for us to read this verse as applying to couples with children, to those without children, and to those whose children are grown. This passage enables us to say that the love of a married couple, in every phase of their lives together, will seek to *give birth* and *give nurture*. If a couple does not have children, or their children have left home, or they marry past the age when they are interested in or able to give birth to children, they will seek other ways to be creative and give of themselves. They may volunteer individually or as a couple in community activities. They may give their time and energy to a social cause they believe in. They may express their creative, nurturing energy through church involvement. All of these are valid ways in which a couple may express the fertile energy of their love.

I have to smile as I observe that couples with children also have this same need to express their creative, nurturing energy. Certainly, a lot of their time and creative energy will be demanded and taken up by corralling and caring for their children. But that wellspring of nurturing vitality needs to be cultivated by involvement outside the family. And especially as children grow older, they benefit from experiencing their family's involvement in social activities, church activities, and community service.

> **God has so composed the body, giving greater honor to the part that lacked it, that there may be no division in the body, but that the members may have the same care for one another. If one member suffers, all suffer together; if one member is honored, all rejoice together. (I Corinthians 12:24-26)**

> **So then, as we have opportunity, let us do good to everyone, and especially to those who are of the household of faith. (Galatians 6:10)**

First Corinthians chapter twelve, verses 24-26, which describes the body of Christ, is commonly interpreted to apply to individual Christians. However, since the term "body" in the text refers to the Christian community, there's no reason the passage shouldn't equally apply to married couples and families. If the word "member" in the text were interpreted to include both individuals and families, the sense would be unchanged. The nurturing energy within a family is not only to be shared between individuals, but between families.

In faithfulness to Scripture therefore, we need to emphasize that Christian married couples will want to give nurture or support to, and receive support from, the other couples in their community. This includes couples in their faith community first (Galatians 6:10), and then couples in their wider community. Christian Marriage cannot be described simply as a tight romantic relationship, or just as a strong nuclear family. A Christian family understands itself as part of a web of families. We are perhaps used to reading Scripture in a way that tells us as individuals what to do for others. But we need to add a second emphasis. The Scripture gives direction to Christian families, telling them to give support, and to open their hearts to accept support from other families in their faith community.

> **Show hospitality to one another without grumbling. (1Peter 4:9)**

> **Greet Apelles, who is approved in Christ. Greet those who belong to the family of Aristobulus. Greet my kinsman Herodion. Greet those in the Lord who belong to the family of Narcissus. (Romans 16:10-11)**

Christian hospitality is important (I Peter 4:9). We have seen that we cannot limit our understanding of hospitality to only hospitality towards individuals. It's also worth noting in this context Paul's final greetings in the book of Romans includes his well-wishes to both individuals and households (Romans 16:10-11). Like Paul, we need to recognize each other's households and put into action our "care for one another" as families.

> **My thoughts are not your thoughts, neither are your ways my ways, declares the Lord. For as the heavens are higher than the earth, so are my ways higher than your ways and my thoughts than your thoughts. (Isaiah 55:8-9)**

It's time to shift subjects. We've been talking about the role of hospitality and community service in the life of Christian families. Now we zero in on the emotional and spiritual dynamics within a married couple, between partners. The imagery we're focusing on now comes from the Old Testament metaphor that portrays God's relationship with his people as that between a husband and wife (Isaiah 54:5; Ezekiel 16:8-14). Similar imagery occurs in the New Testament where God's relationship in Jesus with his people is also described as between a husband and wife. See Ephesians 5:25, 32, where we read, "Husbands, love your wives, as Christ loved the church and gave himself up for her. This mystery is profound, and I am saying that it refers to Christ and the church."

One of the fundamental aspects of God's love relationship with his people is that God is unlike us. God doesn't love us because we are like him. God loves and treasures us in our differentness. Loving your marriage partner with a God-like love means learning to value and love the way your partner is different from you. It is natural to be drawn to a life partner with whom we share common interests and instincts. It is even natural to be drawn to a partner who has character qualities supplementary to ours. But romantic love has a strong component of curiosity and fascination. And it is natural to be fascinated by a person whose personality has characteristics opposite to ours. As much as God's kind of love is love for the different, so Christian Marriage challenges life partners to embrace each other with the kind of love that values and treasures the ways in which they are different from each other.

All of us have heard the popular aphorism, "Opposites attract." This principle is illustrated in both Genesis and Ephesians, where marriage is described as a relationship between different sexes, between a man and a woman. A Christian Marriage need not just be between a man and woman. But married love does need to be an essential attraction between two people who are significantly different – different enough to fascinate each other for a lifetime.

In fact, being of opposite sexes may not be enough of a difference to make a marriage work. A relationship between a man and woman whose personalities are too similar may feel almost incestuous. If the love between you and your partner were to feel like your love for a brother or sister, well, let's just say you've gotten off track somewhere. A vibrant Christian married love needs to be based on an attraction between two people whose personalities are not alike. And a love relationship between two people of the same-sex needs to pay attention to the same principle. The one you love enough to marry needs to have a personality style which is different from your own, with characteristics both supplementary and opposite to yours. This is because one important goal of Christian Marriage is to enable both partners to learn to love each other for the ways *they are different*. Fascinating, mysterious, and different.

Here's the interesting and maddening thing about romantic fascination. Persons different enough to fascinate us and win our love may be also uniquely qualified to irritate and even infuriate us. A life partner can do more than complete us with strengths we need – but do not have. They may also provoke us to deal with issues we need to face – but want to avoid. Those wonderful and captivating characteristics which initially fascinated you about your romantic partner may turn into things which drive you to distraction. And even to anger.

This is an important principle. The prevailing myth about romance in our culture is that we are all looking for our soul mate. We can mistakenly start to think we are looking for a partner who is our spiritual twin. It is important for two married people to share the same life values and religious values. It's hard to steer your marriage journey if you don't share the same map (or the same GPS) and plan to head towards the same destination. But the essential nature of a vital romantic love is to reach out and embrace someone whose differences continue to charm and intrigue us.

Behind those charming differences may be very different assumptions about work, or ambition, or feelings. You may find you two have different expectations about how conflict is best expressed and resolved. You may find the person with whom you fell in love has a very different style of communicating their feelings and fighting for what is important to them. Those very differences, which may have initially charmed and attracted us, can become a source of irritation, misunderstanding, and hard feelings. You may find your styles of communication are in sync when it comes to planning dinner and laughing about the events of last night's party. But your styles of communication may be very much out of sync when it comes to expressing deep or difficult feelings.

My wife and I share very similar life and religious values. But I'm kind of an intuitive dreamer. I'm a "go with your gut" kind of guy. If you ask me what we need to do next, I'll engage my imagination to intuit the path ahead. My wife lives more firmly rooted in the real world. She has a strong imagination, too. But her imagination focuses on the real, the concrete, and the practical. If you ask her what to do next, she'll strategize the practical steps of a real project. It turns out our different ways of planning are very complimentary. We've learned to work very well together.

But our emotional styles are not nearly as compatible or harmonious as our fundamental values. I have deep feelings about intangible values and abstract visions of beauty and wonder. I am drawn to potentialities and long for experiences that involve the intersection of fantasy and the possible. I'm a little bit "airy fairy" and used to wonder why my wife couldn't share my strongest feelings. She, on the other hand, has deep feelings about tangible actions and concrete plans. I can tell you what I'd like my house to feel like; but she can tell you how she wants the house to be designed and decorated. She has little use for fantasy and finds wonder in real things and in realizing her plans. I have to admit a list of things to do leaves me feeling cold. I find the deeply practical to be deeply tedious. And she used to wonder why I couldn't share her deepest feelings.

I can't tell you how many arguments we've had that degenerated into: "You don't respect my feelings;" "You don't get me;" and, "Why don't you feel what I feel?" What we've learned is that loving anger becomes our best friend in arguments of emotional misunderstanding.

Be angry and do not sin; do not let the sun go down on your anger. (Ephesians 4:26)

Because understanding is so important, and misunderstanding between people is so easy, Scripture tells couples to give highest priority to working through problems that cause anger and to do it every day before going to bed. The anger that right away deals with the misunderstanding which causes it, avoids sin. So, don't let misunderstanding fester. Make a strong effort to break down communication barriers as they arise. Loving anger gives us the energy to confront problems and keep the lines of communication open.

It is important to understand that positive anger is an expression of love. We could say positive anger is the energy love gives us to confront interpersonal problems, hurt feelings, and betrayals. When our feelings are hurt, we need to use this powerful energy to ask ourselves why we feel hurt, to confront our partner, and talk through the bruised feelings in our relationship.

You can think of anger this way. Experiencing anger is like picking up a gun. The anger itself is like gun powder. It's strong, explosive energy. You might pick up an ancient, emotional blunderbuss and shoot your anger all over the place without hitting anything, spraying your anger everywhere. That doesn't help your hurt feelings. Instead, it likely makes your situation worse. I think you'll admit though, you and I have sometimes done just this. Or, you might pick up an emotional pistol and shoot your anger at your partner. You may want to punish him or her for causing your hurt feelings. This doesn't help you either. It just drives a bigger wedge between the two of you and makes your hurt feelings harder to solve. And yes, we've sometimes done this too. Or, in an act of frustration, (or fear of conflict) we might carefully select an emotional handgun and "shoot ourselves in the foot," or wound ourselves because we can't muster the courage to send our anger where it belongs – with our partner. How many of us are walking around with self-inflicted emotional wounds?

Suppose, instead, you picked up your emotional pistol and aimed your anger at the problem causing the hurt and creating division between you as a couple? Suppose you could get your partner to aim his or her anger at the same problem? Suppose, instead of being angry at each other, you could come together and both be angry at the problem that is getting you down? That's how anger is intended to be used. That's how loving anger works. Loving anger works on solving problems; destructive anger damages everyone it touches.

Scripture calls destructive anger: bitterness, wrath, and malice. We are to avoid these (Ephesians 4:31; Colossians 3:8). However, in one case Scripture calls Jesus' anger: grief (Mark 3:3-5), and in another case calls his anger: zeal (John 2:14–17). Grief can be described as heartache or heartbreak. Zeal can be described as fervent devotion. It is important to note both grief and zeal (or devotion) can be understood as expressions of love. In both Mark chapter three and John chapter two, Jesus employs his anger, that is, his loving anger, in taking positive action to solve problems. Our goal is to also learn to use our anger to take positive, problem solving action.

How might we do this? It's not something easy I can completely explain in a few sentences. But I can point you in the right direction. Let me suggest that when you feel your anger rising, first make the decision to initiate an argument instead of going into silent mode or turning into a grouch. Confronting someone when you feel hurt is hard. It might even seem counterintuitive. You might feel more like swatting your partner in the head with the nearest book than you feel like talking to him or her. But begin with the decision that you will talk.

Talk about what, though? Here's where you begin to use the energy your anger gives you. Use it to examine your feelings so you can determine exactly what hurt lies behind the anger and what actions triggered your pained feelings. Then use your anger energy to put into words, first to yourself in your own mind, how you feel hurt, or violated, or misunderstood. This will not be easy because bruised feelings are vulnerable feelings and hard to express, even to yourself. They are even harder to express to someone whom you feel has hurt you – even if that someone is your loving partner. Perhaps especially when it is your loving partner. And your next task is: engage your partner in a loving argument.

A loving argument is no small trick. The first thing to remember is to avoid saying, "you made me feel . . . ." Anger tends to want to attack and place blame. Don't do it. Use all your anger energy to help your partner understand exactly the hurt you feel. You may be inclined to think that if your partner really loved you they'd already understand your hurt feelings. Don't go there. This is exactly the time to remember you love your partner because he or she is different from you. He or she likely has a different set of emotional responses to life and a different style of communication. As patiently and as clearly as possible, explain the pain or betrayal or misunderstanding you feel. Help your partner understand what you are experiencing.

The goal of a loving argument is to create understanding, not to retaliate. Use "I statements." Say, "I feel:" and name the feeling. Feelings are not thoughts or judgments. "I feel you are being callous or disrespectful," is a thought or judgment, not a feeling. The feeling might be hurt or betrayal or anger. Begin by putting your thoughts and judgments on hold. You'll likely find your judgments seem less important once you feel understood. So, first name your feelings. Perhaps suggest your partner recall a time when you both experienced a similar feeling together. Step one to healing emotional hurts is to ensure you two understand each other's feelings.

Let me paraphrase from earlier in this chapter. A person who is different enough to fascinate you and win your love is likely to be uniquely qualified to irritate and even infuriate you. Those wonderful and captivating characteristics that initially fascinated you about your romantic partner may turn into things which drive you to distraction and even to anger. But it is the task of Christian love to build bridges of understanding, in times of both harmony and conflict, between yourself and that wonderful, fascinating, and maddening man or woman to whom you gave your heart to love for a lifetime.

Warmly in Christ,

Steve

The Rev. Steve R. Wigall, Th.M., Th.D.

Lawrence, Massachusetts

How irreverent are the stiff and stuffy!
Who is less Godly than those who reject joy and laughter?
Who dishonors the Creator more than those who refuse to be earthy?
How wild and beautiful our God – who is in love with all creation and every person!
Who can keep God's love from healing human hearts with celestial laughter and joy?

LESSON FOUR

DISCUSSION QUESTIONS

Class Opening

(Leader) Gracious God, (pray in unison) **teach us to love each other as a couple with a Christ-like love. Teach us to know each other as Christ knows us. Teach us to take joy in each other as Christ takes joy in us.**

When love gets hard, let us be patient with each other as you are patient. Let us strive to be understanding as you understand. Let us be faithful to each other as you are faithful.

Grant that through our shared successes and failures, through our shared happiness and sorrow, we might find lasting joy in the lessons of love which you teach us. We pray in the name of Jesus Christ, who shows us your love, calls us to love, and empowers us with your love. Amen

The Discipline of Family Love: 6 – 9

6. **Involve the one you love in your family.**

Married love is not just a private matter between two people. At its heart, it involves expanding family ties and extending the reach of a family's love to include new people. Couples need to share their lives and their love with members of their extended families.

(Song of Solomon 8:2)

Questions to discuss:

1. What questions do you have from the Couple's Pamphlet or from the Couple's Letter(s)? Ask the couple or couples, "Is there homework from our last session? Are there questions that have come to your mind since we last met or talked?" Share homework.

2. Do your parents extend to you the right to marry the person you love and to bring that person into their extended family? How do they express their welcome or rejection?

3. Would you freely welcome into your family the person your child chooses to marry? What might cause you to withhold your blessing or welcome? Be patient and forgiving if either of your in-laws do not welcome your marriage. How would you feel about politely avoiding them, while hoping their attitude will change? Is there another approach to unwelcoming in-laws which you might take?

4. How do you feel about including your parents and in-laws in the extended family formed by your marriage? How would you feel should your parents resist being included in your family or circumstances (such as distance) make this impossible?

7.   Find ways to give creative expression to your love.

All families need to find ways to express their love. This can involve parenting children and nurturing social causes. It certainly will involve giving support to and receiving support from other families in the Christian faith community.

(Psalms 128:3; I Corinthians 12:24-26; Romans 16:10-11; I Peter 4:9)

Questions to discuss:

5. Married love is essentially nurturing and creative. How do you feel about making it a first priority in your life to nurture your partner? Can you imagine giving yourself to nurture your partner, not only without losing yourself, but actually becoming more yourself?

6. What interests do you both support as a couple that energize you both?

7. What are ways you as a couple would enjoy giving yourselves to others, to the church, to your community?

8.   Learn how to love someone who is different.

It is natural to be drawn to a life partner who has a supplementary. and even opposite, personality characteristics. Christian Marriage challenges life partners to embrace each other with the kind of love that values and treasures a person for the ways in which they are different.

See Isaiah 55:8-9, which says, "My thoughts are not your thoughts, neither are your ways my ways, declares the Lord."

Questions to discuss:

8. What likes, preferences and instincts do you see in yourself that you do not see in your partner? What strengths do you see in your partner you do not see in yourself?

9. Give examples of situations in which the two of you would have made different decisions or responded very differently.

10. Can you imagine learning to enjoy each other's differences?

11. Are your worship preferences similar and compatible?

12. Have you discussed how you would want to handle the religious training of your children? How is the vision you have for the religious training of children, should you have them, similar or not similar?

9.   Expect love to provoke you to grow and change.

Persons different enough to fascinate us and win our love may provoke and even infuriate us. A life partner can do more than complete us with strengths we need – but do not have. They will also provoke us to deal with issues we need to face – but want to avoid.

(Ephesians 4:26)

<u>Questions to discuss</u>:

13. Why might it be better to judge the strength of your romantic relationship on the quality of your arguments rather than on the passion of your intimacy?

14. Is it your goal to avoid argument or to develop together the skill of loving and helpful argument?

15. Discuss the following outline of a strategy for loving argument.

    - If you can feel your anger rising and realize that you are about to initiate an argument in your relationship, decide to use the energy your anger gives you to determine exactly what you feel and what actions triggered those negative feelings.

    - Put in words to yourself how you feel hurt, or violated, or misunderstood. This will not be easy because bruised feelings are vulnerable feelings and hard to express.

    - Use your anger energy to risk expressing your hurt or violated or misunderstood feelings, without placing blame.

    - Then ask for your partner's understanding and empathy.

16. Is it better to resolve an argument with an apology or with understanding? Discuss the following observation. When feelings are wounded, an apology is often not enough. Nothing heals wounded feelings like knowing the one who has hurt you has also put in the effort to understand your hurt – from your point of view.

LESSON FIVE

PERSONAL LETTER TO COUPLES

Dear Precious Couples,

Y ou may have wondered why, in my previous letter to you, I put such a strong emphasis on loving arguments. Why in talking about Christian Marriage and *The Discipline of Family Love*,

would I so heavily highlight the elements of struggle and conflict? Let me share with you my favorite marriage advice. If there was only one thing I could say to every couple seeking Christian Marriage, I'd tell them this. Your happiness as a married couple doesn't so much depend on your ability to have fun together, or have great sex, it depends on your ability to lovingly argue. This advice comes from my personal experience and my work with many couples over the years. But this advice also comes from my study of Scripture.

In explaining how this advice comes from Scripture, I'll pinpoint for you specific Scripture verses. But I also want to point out the lessons we can gain from examining the broad historical sweep of God's developing relationship with humanity. Let me begin by suggesting we could perfectly describe Scripture's story of the human relationship with God as a long, ongoing, loving conflict or argument (because of sin), that finally ends happily with peace and reconciliation (because of Christ) taking the place of hard feelings and estrangement. It's the story of a love relationship between two very different parties (God and humanity), who entered into a phase of conflict and estrangement but ended with a healed and restored relationship.

At the beginning of our human relationship with God, we had a major falling out with our loving Creator – so we read in the opening chapters of Genesis. Over the ages of biblical history, God repeatedly reached out to us trying to win us back. Our history with God is one of struggle and conflict which concludes with Christ breaking down all the walls of anger and hurt separating us from God and restoring the loving harmony with God we had lost. I'm going to try to show you how the story of God's loving struggle with humanity provides us with a perfect template for understanding our own loving relationships with each other – especially the loving relationship of Christian Marriage.

As the Bible tells us about God's love, it realistically portrays the gen-eral dynamics of love. My suggestion is that, as the Bible tells the story of God's struggle with humanity, a story of conflict and ultimate resolution, it sheds light on the dynamics of married love. In an earlier letter, I've shared with you that love draws us to someone different from ourselves. In this letter, I'll describe how love that brings us together then throws down the gauntlet. It challenges us to learn to love this marvelous and strange, and yes sometimes vexing and irritating person.

I believe you'll find, if you can learn to fight and struggle and stay on the same side, then the blessings and joys of married love can open up for you. If you don't learn to stay on the same side, then the fighting and struggle that life inevitably brings every couple, can explode like a bomb within your relationship. The result may well be damaged and hurt feelings. The result might even be an end to your love and the end of your marriage itself. My goal in this letter is to begin giving your love the tools to lovingly argue, survive, and thrive. This will just be an introductory primer. The real course work will take place within your marriage.

1)   The first principle in handling conflict in marriage is to remember to focus on your early love, a time when harmony and joy prevailed. It's not by accident the story of Scripture begins in a garden para-dise with a relationship of perfect harmony between a loving God and God's two beloved humans. Whenever there is discord in the divine / human relationship, the Eden story calls us to remember a time when

harmony and joy prevailed between ourselves and God. In the same way, when there is discord in our marriages, we are called to remember the "Eden time" in our relationship, when harmony and joy prevailed between us. Whatever the upset, the hurt, or the drama you are going through, never take your eyes off the goal of recapturing and even deepening your first couple love.

When you find yourself in the middle of an argument, or you are seriously unhappy with each other, it can greatly help you to recall and get in touch with the joy you had at the beginning of your relationship. You need to see beyond your present emotional pain and look back on your good times. This can enable you to get through the hard and painful feelings you are facing, and give you hope for your future together. But what if you are unable to find your way back to your original couple joy? What if these memories have gone dark? What if they seem too far away to be recaptured? Then challenge yourself to go *forward to a new joy* that can build on the totality of your couple experiences. This may take some serious imagination. But you'll never get past your present pain by focusing *only* on your problems and hurt feelings. Give your imagination a major work out and conjure up a new set of dreams, you as an individual can strive for, and you as a couple can share.

When you get into an argument, the temptation is to want to win. The temptation is to focus on vindicating yourself. To actually "win" at a loving argument, you need to realize the only one who needs to win is *your relationship.* The only one who needs vindicating is *your marriage*. As much as you may feel an argument pits you against each other, you need to both fight on the same side to make your marriage the winner. As I said in the last lesson, you can think of your frustration and anger as a gun. The thing to remember is to not aim your gun at your partner. Be frustrated. Be angry. But aim the gun of your frustration and anger at the problem separating you. Attack, but not each other. Attack the cause of your hurt and resentment. Fight, but fight for your marriage. We'll be talking more about how to do this.

85

2)   The second principle involved in handling conflict in your marriage is to always seek reconciliation. Always work to restore the peace between yourselves. The scriptural model of seeking reconciliation is the cross of Jesus. On the cross, God is at work to restore peace between ourselves and him. Let's look at the story of the crucifixion to see how God goes about seeking reconciliation with us. How does God go about making peace with humanity? Paul introduces the New Testament principle of reconciliation in Romans 5:11-12.

> **For if while we were enemies we were reconciled to God by the death of his Son, much more, now that we are reconciled, shall we be saved by his life. More than that, we also rejoice in God through our Lord Jesus Christ, through whom we have now received reconciliation.**

How does the "death of his son" reconcile us to God? Lots of strange and strained theories have been put forward to explain human reconciliation with God. I'll not go into these. Instead, I'll ask us to think of our relationship with God as a love relationship strained to the breaking point. I'll ask us to consider what God says to us on the cross that ends our estranged relationship, mends fences between us, and finally reunites us.

Consider that God was in Christ, revealing himself to us (see John 1:14). Through everything Jesus said and did, God was saying to us, "This is what I am like. This is what is in my heart." The central conviction of Christian faith is that the cross is God's supreme act of love and self-disclosure. What does God's love say to us from the cross? The most obvious message is, "I suffer. My love suffers. I am with you; and for me, this means pain."

How does this message reconcile us to God? Consider what one person can say to another to break down walls of resentment and hurt feelings. Anger doesn't do it. On the cross, God isn't saying to humanity, I'm mad at you. The hurt feelings between a couple are not overcome by the one who is hurt being angry. Neither does judgment do it.

On the cross, God isn't saying to humanity, I judge you as guilty. The solution to hurt couple feelings isn't helped by the one who feels hurt calling the other one bad names and slinging judgments at them. To overcome the hurt feelings that divide us, we need to take a counter-intuitive step. Reconciliation begins when the person who feels most hurt chooses to become vulnerable. On the cross, God becomes vulnerable to us. On the cross, God says to us, in fact shows us, "This is now badly I am hurting."

When a human relationship has been damaged, one of the parties, in the midst of their pain, has to choose to be vulnerable enough to say, "Let me tell you how badly I am hurting." This choice to be vulnerable means deciding to set aside anger and judgment, and to express so the other person can understand just how devastated and anguished you feel. It means expressing your hurt feelings without anger. It means expressing your hurt feelings without judgment. Don't put your partner on the defensive. Don't place blame.

Remember anger erupts out of our experience of feeling hurt and wronged. Your erupting anger may feel like a flame thrower with which you want to incinerate your partner. Resist that urge. You may feel so wronged you want to explode onto your partner with labels of judgment, calling them every bad name you can think of. Refrain from that. Instead, choose to be vulnerable and explain as clearly as you can just how badly you feel wounded. Explain your pain. And remember, use neither anger, nor judgment, nor blame.

A wounded love relationship is healed when the person who has done wrong understands the magnitude of the hurt they caused and undergoes a change of heart that allows them to see their relationship differently. This is what God does for us with Jesus on the cross. God sets aside anger and judgment and shows us how deeply he feels hurt. Because God loves us so deeply, when we turn our backs on him and wander into self-destructive, ego-centered, and pain-laden paths, God is hurt. When our lives batter us with suffering, God suffers with us.

Because God loves us, he is never distant from us. God always wants us to be wrapped in his love and joy and peace. So when we wander from Him, God's heart is wounded. When our life path brings us sorrow or loss God grieves and mourns with us. God is pained by our rejections and wounded whenever the thorns of life scar and tear at us.

This is God's message to us on the cross, and it is the path to seeking reconciliation when a couple experiences hurt feelings. The one of you most hurt has to set aside their anger and judgment, and as clearly as possible, communicate how badly they feel. Healing comes about when the dividing wall of pain and resentment is replaced by empathy. If you feel hurt, what do you most want? Does it really make you feel better if the person who hurt you feels guilty? No, you probably think they should feel guilty. Does it make you feel better if the person who hurt you begs for your forgiveness? No, why should you forgive? Does it make you feel better if the person who hurt you buys you things or does nice stuff for you? Well, that's distracting; but it doesn't heal your hurt.

Empathy is the only thing that can heal wounded feelings. When your partner has done something to hurt you, what you want them to do is listen respectfully to your feelings, to understand what you're going through, and to let you know that they understand the depth of your pain. You want them to deeply "get" what you're feeling and to be changed by their new and clearer understanding of the turmoil and upset you've experienced. This is empathetic understanding; and it is the only thing that can heal wounded feelings, and reconcile a damaged relationship.

Similarly, our broken relationship with God is rekindled when we "get" how deeply and passionately God loves us and suffers with us; when we realize God's love is not a distant abstraction but the most intimate of realities. When God's love comes alive for us, and we open our hearts to trust and know God's love as a daily necessity, as essential to us as the air we breathe, our relationship with God is healed.

3)   The third principle involved in handling conflict in your marriage is to realize that empathy leads to confession. Confession is the action or behavior that expresses empathy. It's interesting that Christians tend to think when we sin, we ought to ask for forgiveness or pray for God's mercy. The old Christian prayer called the Jesus prayer, commonly used by both Catholic and Orthodox Christians, is a prayer for God's mercy. The prayer's words, in English, are: "Lord Jesus Christ, Son of God, have mercy on me, a sinner."

However, Scripture never links God's forgiveness or reconciliation with God either with asking for forgiveness for our sins or praying for God's mercy. Scripture primarily teaches that we gain God's complete forgiveness through faith. But Scripture also tells us to confess. Both Orthodox and Catholic churches have a sacrament of confession. I suggest, though, that confession is a spiritual principle which is more essential than what takes place inside a confessional with a priest inside a church. We need to ask ourselves just what confession of sin means and does. I suggest it both maintains our relationship with God and heals that relationship when it becomes strained. I suggest we'll find confession is also the most direct and most powerful means of healing our marriage relationships when they become strained or conflicted.

Confession of our sin to God is taught in I John 1:9. In that epistle, we read: "If we confess our sins, he (God) is faithful and just to forgive us our sins and to cleanse us from all unrighteousness." In the initial chapter of John's first epistle, the topic of conversation is maintaining a strong and open relationship or fellowship with God. This theme is expressed in the third verse of this chapter: "That which we have seen and heard we proclaim also to you, so that you too may have *fellowship* with us; and indeed our *fellowship* is with the Father and with his Son Jesus Christ." What the author is teaching is how to maintain strong Christian relationships (fellowship), both with God and with our fellow Christians.

We are fully reconciled to God when we open our hearts in faith to trust God's love for us. This section of I John is not talking about our reconciliation with God. In fact, in every other place, Scripture makes it clear we are forgiven and reconciled to God by faith. I John is discussing something different. Even though the word forgiveness is used here, the topic is not God's acceptance of us – sin and all. Forgiveness here means something more limited. It means maintaining the strength and openness of a Christian relationship (i.e. fellowship), primarily with God but also with each other. This we do by confessing those sins that burden or break those relationships. We are forgiven by the faith that trusts God's love. But this second kind of forgiveness involves maintaining the closeness of that loving relationship. We maintain love relationships with God and with each other by confessing our sins.

Exactly what does confessing our sin involve? Confessing our sin is different from but similar to elocution in court. Elocution is what a defendant does when pleading guilty. He or she stands before the judge and says what he or she has done wrong. Similarly, confession in Scripture is something we say before God. But it is more than saying what we've done wrong. It is self-judgment. Self-judgment is an important method which the New Testament teaches us for handling our sins. The principal passage where self-judgment is discussed is in I Corinthians chapter eleven. The primary relevant verse is I Corinthians 11:31. I paraphrase: If we judge ourselves properly God will not need to judge or discipline us.

Self-judgment and confession are nearly identical concepts. The Greek word translated confess in I John, chapter one, (homologeo, in the infinitive) means to agree, or to be of one mind, or to say the same thing. In the context of the first epistle of John, the meaning is to judge ourselves as we believe God would. It means trying to be one mind with God about ourselves and or behavior. It means saying to God the same thing we judge God would say to us about our actions. Elocution is just admitting the wrong we've done. Confession involves using our empathy to see ourselves as God might see us, and then to exercise self-judgment, on the basis of our empathy, to express to God the insight we've gained about ourselves.

This principle works the same way between Christians and especially between loving marriage partners. When one has sinned against the other by causing hurt feelings, begging for forgiveness may be our first instinct. But begging for forgiveness is the easy way out. Saying we are sorry is also too easy. Neither actually costs us anything. Unfortunately, most of the times we ask for forgiveness or say we are sorry, we are merely trying to get our partner to stop being mad at us. Healing hurt feelings within a marriage requires of us doing something harder. It requires us to take responsibility for what we've done. It requires us to employ our empathy to judge ourselves the way our partner is judging us. It tells our partner we've done the hard work of understanding the full impact of the hurt we've caused them.

If this is a new idea for you, let me say it can revolutionize your relationships. It can bring healing to emotional wounds that might otherwise seem insurmountable. It can reopen the doors to love when those doors seem to have closed. When we learn to use the magic of empathy, we learn to see our actions from the viewpoint of the loved one we have hurt. Then by confession, we learn to have the toughness and courage to tell that person what we see in ourselves. It takes courage to look at ourselves from our partner's point of view, to agree with their view, and to then tell them we now see ourselves differently. It takes tough love to give your partner the gift of your understanding and empathy. This is confession. Confession is a direct expression of empathy. And it has the power to bring reconciliation in the midst of the most strained relationship.

4)   The fourth and final principle involved in handling conflict in your marriage involves embracing the joy of self-revelation. Love takes pleasure in revealing itself and rejoices in the revealing of its partner. Battling through the strains and reconciliations, learning to

exercise empathy, and offering the gift of hard won understanding, these things offer life's greatest and most intense opportunity for two people to deeply experience the joys marriage can offer.

Let me observe that the Old and New Testaments taken together, are the story of God's continued efforts at self-disclosure. When we, as Christians, learn to see that God is love, we learn to see the story of Scripture as the ongoing expression of God's love for us and the narrative of God's continuous effort to reveal himself. The joy in marital love similarly comes from self-revelation. It is the joy of doing the hard work of learning to know, and of making ourselves known to, the one person we've committed to love for a lifetime. When the story of *your* Christian Marriage is finally told, it will be a story of the battles, the upheavals, and the circumstances through which you made yourselves known to each other.

Let's look now at how Scripture tells the story of God revealing himself to us. I want to point out it's taken millennium for God to slowly disclose himself to humanity. I want us to remember God is a complex being. God as a Person, is multifaceted, multilayered, and endlessly mysterious. Our joy at getting to know God won't be exhausted by eternity. The process of getting to know God won't ever be cut short or lose its inherent joyfulness.

I point this out because so often human love begins at its outset, during dating or early marriage, with the thrilling feeling we've known this person for a lifetime. We gaze on this precious person and may feel a sense of almost immediate recognition. *Soul mate* we may call them. The more mystical minded among us may claim to be so deeply connected to their loved one they say they've known each other in past lives. We humans are not as complicated or complex as is God. But we humans are created in God's image; and I suggest we are all mysteries. It is not an overstatement to suggest getting to know another person is not a matter of instant recognition. It can easily take a lifetime of hard work. Too often married partners give up on each other because they think they already know what each other can and cannot do. In this life, we are all beginners at the joyful struggle of "getting to know you."

Consider the long and gradual story of humanity getting to know God. In Genesis, God's initial self-disclosure was as Creator. To Abraham, God was the one who called him to leave home and follow and promised to bless his family. To Jacob, God was the one with whom he wrestled all night and who promised to make his descendants into a strong nation. To Joseph, God was the one who rescued him from slavery and prison and used him to bless both the nation of Egypt and his eleven brothers. To Moses, God was YHWH, who revealed himself as: "I am who I am" (Exodus 3:14); and as the one who led the nation of Israel on the road to Exodus and freedom. To the people of Israel wandering in the wilderness, God was a guide in the form of a cloud by day and a pillar of fire by night. God gave Israel a unique message about himself through Moses in the three forms of Law: Moral, Civil, and Judicial. During and after the rule of King David, God made himself known as reigning King of Creation. To the Jewish prophets of the later kingdom, God showed himself as the King who desired to reign in mercy and justice.

But today, the New Testament gives us an ultimate and complete self-revelation of God in the man Jesus (Hebrews 1:3). The self-disclosure of God in Jesus shows us the glory of God the Father (John 1:14). When we look at Christ, we see God. And when the light of God shines in our hearts, we are able to experience the knowledge of God's glory shining within us from the person of Christ (II Corinthians 4:4-6). A Christian may indeed say he or she knows God. And that seed of the knowledge of God may have truly been planted in our hearts and minds. But the tree of that knowledge will never stop growing throughout eternity.

There are important lessons for Christian married couples to learn from God's story of making himself known to us. Let me state the first lesson as a simple syllogism. Salvation is about getting to know God (e.g. John 17:3). Salvation is also about joy (e.g. Psalm 51:12; Luke 2:10). So, getting to know God is also about joy. The first lesson for Christian couples is that the process of "getting to know" someone special, like God, like your marriage partner, is a joyful process. Many days it may just seem like work. Many days that work may seem vexing or tedious. But in the long run, knowing that one special person yields joy. I'm even going to suggest there is nothing that yields as much continued joy as taking a long time to develop a deep knowledge of a special, wonderful person.

That brings us to the second lesson. The joy available to a Christian married couple from working to know each other is a joy that has a present reality that only increases over the long haul. The joy may shine during special moments of intimacy. But it's a joy a couple builds together one day at a time, one struggle at a time, one battle at a time, one crisis at a time, and one intimacy at a time. The joy inherent in self-disclosure and the discovery of your spouse is one that grows slowly over the days and years of living through everything life and relationship throws at you.

So, let me assure you precious couples who are reading these letters and studying these lessons, that seeking reconciliation is worth your effort. Doing the work to develop empathy and understanding is worth your effort. Facing couple conflict with honest confession and self-judgment is far from easy, but is worth your effort. It is worth it for a Christian married couple because the resulting self-disclosure and mutual discovery produces the blossoming knowledge, that daily and long term, yields the greatest of life's joys.

In this letter, I've emphasized conflict and reconciliation. That's because joy is built in these moments. But that joy is lived out and enjoyed as a wonderful blanket that increasingly wraps itself around a couple when they are at work, when they are making breakfast, when they are doing laundry, or when they are washing floors, wiping down counters, and working in their yard. In the beginning of marriage, you do special things together to feel that special, dare I say, romantic, couple joy. After years of building empathy and understanding in the face of life's ups and downs, that same special couple joy attaches itself to the mundane. The small and trivial become wrapped in an aura of, dare I say, romantic specialness. When reading a book, helping a child with homework, working on a hobby, and getting dressed in the morning become romantic and special, the hard work of getting to know each other pays off in daily joy.

That joy is what I wish for each of you.

Warmly in Christ,

$\mathcal{S}teve$

The Rev. Steve R. Wigall, Th.M., Th.D.

Lawrence, Massachusetts

How irreverent are the stiff and stuffy!
Who is less Godly than those who reject joy and laughter?
Who dishonors the Creator more than those who refuse to be earthy?
How wild and beautiful our God – who is in love with all creation and every person!
Who can keep God's love from healing human hearts with celestial laughter and joy?

LESSON FIVE

DISCUSSION QUESTIONS

Class Opening

> (Leader) Gracious God, (pray in unison) **teach us to love each other as a couple with a Christ-like love. Teach us to know each other as Christ knows us. Teach us to take joy in each other as Christ takes joy in us.**
>
> **When love gets hard, let us be patient with each other as you are patient. Let us strive to be understanding as you understand. Let us be faithful to each other as you are faithful.**
>
> **Grant that through our shared successes and failures, through our shared happiness and sorrow, we might find lasting joy in the lessons of love which you teach us. We pray in the name of Jesus Christ, who shows us your love, calls us to love, and empowers us with your love. Amen**

The Discipline of Family Love: 10

10. Strive to build a lasting love relationship.

Commit yourself to building a lasting love relationship that treasures its first joy; seeks understanding and reconciliation when there is conflict; admits when its actions cause hurt; takes pleasure in mutual self-revelation; and does all it can to foster an enduring bond of honesty and trust.

The following phases or steps describe the process of working through relationship problems as small as a misunderstanding or as large as severely hurt feelings. They describe how a relationship can move from conflict to reconciliation and healing. By regularly working through these steps, a couple can steadily move towards building a strong and lasting love relationship.

(1)   Remember and focus on your early love, when harmony and joy prevailed. Imagine recapturing that time.

Questions to discuss:

1. What questions do you have from the Couple's Pamphlet or from the Couple's Letter(s)? Ask the couple or couples, "Is there homework from our last session? Are there questions that have come to your mind since we last met or talked?" Share homework.

2. When you have had an argument, or serious unhappiness, have you tried recalling and treasuring the joy you had at the beginning of your relationship? Would looking back on good times help you get through hard or painful times?

3. What would it take for you as a couple to remember and recapture your first joy?

4. What if you as a couple are not able to go back to your original joy? This need not be a loss. Discuss the following statement. You can challenge yourselves to go *forward to a new joy* that can account for and build on the totality of your experiences.

(2)   Seek reconciliation.

Questions to discuss:

5. When, if ever, might your promises to "mend your ways" help your love relationship grow?

6. When, if ever, might your willingness to give your partner sincere flattery, unexpected praise, and surprise gifts, help your love relationship grow?

7. Do such behaviors help more when you are trying to heal bruised feelings, or when done out of a generous heart when things are going well in your marriage relationship?

(3)   Reconciliation begins with building understanding.

Questions to discuss:

8. When your feelings are hurt how do you feel when your partner apologizes and says, "I'm sorry?"

9. Discuss the following observation. Healing empathy cannot take place unless the person who is hurt expresses, clearly, calmly, and without placing blame, the pain they feel.

10. When your feelings are hurt, how would you feel if your partner listens empathetically, communicates they understand the depth of your hurt, and lets you know they are willing to be changed by their understanding?

(4)   Offer confession and extend empathy.

Questions to discuss:

11. We first learn to argue from our parents, then later from our friends and loved ones. Can you give an example of an important argument which you witnessed or were involved in that was ended by understanding and empathy?

12. Can you give an example of an important argument in which your complaint was met by confession?

13. What makes it hard for you to think about what you have said or done from your partner's viewpoint, see how you have caused hurt, and then tell your partner what you've discovered about yourself? (Confession)

14. When you have hurt the one you love, and catch yourself doing it, or your loved one confronts you with their hurt, what is your first response? What might your best response be?

(5) Embrace the joy of self-revelation.

Questions to discuss:

15. Is the "getting to know you" stage of your marriage relationship over, or is it something that still keeps giving you joy? What has triggered a recent "getting to know you" moment?

16. Identify what you struggle with when you try to disclose yourself (your feelings, thoughts, and convictions) to your partner?

17. What is the most effective thing you have learned to do to help your partner reveal themselves (their feelings, thoughts, and convictions) to you?

18. Discuss the following observation. Love takes pleasure in revealing itself and rejoices in the revealing of its partner.

LESSON SIX

PERSONAL LETTER TO COUPLES

Dear Precious Couples,

We're coming to the end of our discussions and I'll soon be sending you out to get busy with the laboratory part of the course: your marriage. In the last letter and this one, I'm explaining just how the beating heart of *The Discipline of Family Love* involves trust and honesty. Trust and honesty are the lifeblood of both the Christian relationship with God and a vibrant Christian Marriage. In this way, there is important similarity between the human love relationship with God and the love shared by married couples.

For example, the hallmark of Protestant Christianity is the conviction that our salvation relationship with God is born and lives by our faith and trust in God. We call this conviction: salvation by faith. It means that our willingness to place our faith in God undergirds our relationship with God. Similarly, our willingness as married couples to put our faith in each other undergirds our married love. A couple's faith in each other is enshrined at the moment in the wedding service when we say to each other, "I do."

How is it an expression of faith when a couple holds hands, looks into each other's eyes, and promises, "I do?" Consider the historic English wedding vow. It makes explicit that the couple's promise is to place their faith or trust in each other. The archaic wording is, "I *plight* thee *my troth*." The verb, "plight," means "to pledge." The phrase "my troth" means: "*my faith.*" The couples being married are vowing to each other, "I pledge you ***my faith*** (and faithfulness). I pledge my *personal fidelity* to you. In effect, "I promise *to be true* to you; you can **trust** me."

In my last letter to you, I explained that life will trip each of us up causing big and small moments of hurt and betrayal. When feelings are hurt, when trust feels broken, both parties in a marriage relationship will want to work towards reconciliation, using the skills we discussed: empathy, understanding, and confession. These skills embody the value of **honesty**.

There are two important kinds of honesty essential to Christian Marriage. Interestingly, the New Testament Scripture uses the word "confess" to express both of these kinds of honesty. We've already discussed that confess means to honestly self-judge (as in confess your sins). But it also means to honestly profess (as in express your convictions). A strong love relationship with God and with your marriage partner requires both kinds of honesty: confession and profession. Honesty plays these two roles: the honesty to face and discuss the wrongs we've done; and the honesty to profess or share our deepest feelings, convictions and values. Honest confession heals relationships by applying empathy to bruised feelings. Profession is the kind of honesty that continually opens the heart to build bridges of understanding with those it loves by sharing with them its deepest feelings and values.

Trust, translated as "believe," and honesty, described as "confess," is used in Romans 10:9-10, to describe our salvation relationship with God. In these verses, Paul uses the word translated into English as "confess" to mean what we'd usually describe as "profess."

> **If you confess with your mouth that Jesus is Lord and believe in your heart that God raised him from the dead, you will be saved. For with the heart one believes and is justified, and with the mouth one confesses and is saved.**

Believing in the sense described in these verses refers to the trust that makes our relationships real and lasting. The kind of profession described in these verses involves the honest sharing of our most important, heartfelt convictions and persuasions. The word "saved" as used in these verses could refer to our eternal salvation. But the word can also mean to be kept safe or to last. Since I'm talking to you about how our love relationship with God can parallel our marital love, I suggest the meaning of "saved" for a married couple has more of this second meaning for our love to be kept safe and for our marriages to last. If I were to paraphrase these verses to show how they apply to a married couple, I would say something like:

> **If you honestly profess with your mouth your deepest and truest feelings and convictions in conversation with your partner, and trust in your heart that your partner is good and worthy, your marriage will last. For with the heart you trust, enabling your love to grow; with the mouth you honestly professes your deepest thoughts and feelings, enabling your marriage to last.**

We previously discussed how hard it can be to talk about our feelings of hurt and pain. Such honest self-critical sharing requires the decision to risk being vulnerable. But putting your most treasured values and convictions into words and sharing them also requires risk and vulnerability. The vulnerability involves sharing our most important thoughts. The risk is we might not be understood or accepted.

How do I suggest you as couples go about sharing your important personal thoughts and feelings? First, accept that significant sharing will be much harder than small talk and harder than strategically planning daily or weekly schedules. Give yourselves a block of unhurried time to talk, and clear out a comfortable spot where you won't be interrupted. Parents busy raising small children can find this challenging. So can couples where one party is working against a deadline, or is consumed by a work related project. Because all of us are busy, it can help us to make a habit of scheduling talking dates. Whether you schedule talking dates daily, weekly, monthly, or as needed, putting times to talk on your schedule can be essential. Waiting for a good time to spontaneously appear can be a cause of serious frustration. Your love is not in trouble if time for serious personal sharing does not materialize effortlessly. Don't be frustrated. It just means life has happened to you; you are busy. I suggest you'll need to get used to having to schedule dates for romantic times together. And you'll need to get used to having to schedule dates for serious talking.

One important point about scheduling times for serious discussion. Please don't try to schedule serious talks just before bedtime unless absolutely necessary. One or both of you will probably be way too mentally and/or emotionally exhausted. To really open your heart, and really listen, takes energy. It's far better to schedule talking time when your energy is fresher. By all means, schedule times to go out to dinner and a movie when it fits into your budget. But if there are unresolved issues and conflicted feelings floating in the air around you, neither of you will be emotionally present to enjoy the date. You will need regular times for serious conversation. For this, you might consider scheduling weekend breakfast times or setting aside time for morning walks together.

If you as a couple don't observe a regularly set aside time for talking, then I suggest you'll need to give yourselves permission to ask, "I need a talking date. May we schedule one?" And I'll suggest one other tool that can facilitate times of significant sharing. Write a letter to your partner and give it to them when you schedule your talking time. Deep feelings and convictions can be hard to put into words. It can help your partner understand you better, if you first take the time to find the right words to express yourself. This is especially true if your personal thoughts and feelings are bringing up an area of disagreement, or unmet need.

A couple of guidelines for writing a letter to begin a discussion. Begin with saying something that puts you and your partner in a positive mood. Begin with telling your partner something you love about him or her. Say, "In recent days, I've noticed you do this really nice thing." Tell them what the nice thing is. Then say, "I love this about you." Then as you jump into what you want to share, make a clear distinction between your thoughts and your feelings. Say, "I feel," only when describing one of your emotions. Say, "I think" or "I judge," to introduce one of your thoughts, convictions, or conclusions. Saying, "I feel *that,*" almost always means you are expressing a thought and not a feeling. It can really help facilitate communication between you as a couple if you keep clear the distinction between your thoughts and feelings.

Even if the personal feeling or conviction you want to discuss is about a disagreement or unmet need, don't attack. If your partner feels defensive, they will not be able to listen to you or hear anything you say about your feelings. Their minds will be busy thinking about defending themselves. Say, "I feel, to express your emotions; and I think, to express your thoughts and judgments." To clearly express yourself, try saying something like, "When you do that thing, I feel this." Speak only for yourself. Also don't explain to your partner what they feel or think. Expressing yourself is hard enough without trying to be a mind reader. It will be a big help for both of you to increasingly distinguish the real person to whom you are married from the image of your partner which you have in your minds. Remember human beings are holy mysteries. The longer you live together and love each other, the less certain you will be that you know your partner. His or her ability to surprise you will grow over time, not diminish.

My point is, the kind of couple honesty and intimacy that shares deep thoughts and feelings is not likely to happen accidentally. You'll need to be intentional about it. Plan for talking dates. Prepare for them. Sometimes you'll want to write your partner a letter to facilitate easier and clearer communication. Getting to deeply know that special person is one of life's greatest joys, and that will mean doing the work of opening your heart to them.

In my personal letters to you, I've discussed how *The Discipline of Family Love* finds its basis in Scripture. In conclusion, I want to brief-ly survey how the definition of Christian Marriage is also founded on Scripture. I'll list the Scripture passages I'm drawing from and briefly comment on each one.

1. **Then the man said, "This at last is bone of my bones and flesh of my flesh; she shall be called Woman, because she was taken out of Man." Therefore a man shall leave his father and his mother and hold fast to his wife, and they shall become one flesh. (Genesis 2:23-24)**

It's interesting, as we read through Scripture, that marriage is often discussed but weddings are mentioned infrequently. In Genesis 2:24, the wedding of Adam and Eve is not described. Instead, an initial rationale for marriage is given. It's essentially a procreative rationale. It's also interesting to note who is talking in this verse. Either Adam is talking in continuation of his comments in verse 23 and offering his understanding of his own marriage. Or the author of Genesis is talking, offering his understanding of marriage.

Genesis 2:24 is sometimes interpreted as a God-given definition of marriage. But let's be honest in our dealing with the Genesis text. In a later passage, in Genesis 3:16-24, God directly speaks to Adam and Eve as husband and wife. He gives them both instructions. Genesis 2:24 is different. This verse is not spoken in God's voice and cannot be God's instructions to the first couple. God knows Adam and Eve have no need to leave their fathers or mothers; they do not have par-ents. This observation about procreative marriage is inserted in the Garden narrative, either in the telling or the writing of the Creation story. I suggest we take it seriously that Genesis does not attribute this comment to God. I further suggest, in faithfulness to the text, we in-terpret these words to be descriptive of an early human understanding of marriage inserted by Genesis' author, and not intended to be God's once and for all prescription for marriage. The voice speaking in these verses is simply not God's voice.

2. **And the man and his wife were both naked and were not ashamed. (Genesis 2:25).**

   And they heard the sound of the LORD God walking in the garden in the cool of the day, and the man and his wife hid themselves from the presence of the LORD God among the trees of the garden. (Genesis 3:8)

In Genesis 2:25 and in Genesis 3:8, Adam and Eve are described as man and wife, as a married couple. But their wedding isn't described here either.

I suggest the first couple are essentially married by agreeing to "hold fast" to each other, as described in Genesis 2:24, with God as their witness. No one else was present with them in the Garden to witness their marriage, neither was anyone else needed. They entered into marriage by uniting or joining their lives together in the sight of God. I suggest our understanding of Christian Marriage has to start here. Marriage begins when two people stand before God, and pledge their lives to each other, promising to unite their lives in loving commitment. A Christian wedding celebrates this pledge by reenacting it, and solemnizes it by performing it before the Christian community. A Christian wedding gives the couple the gift of recognizing their marriage and welcoming them as married members of the faith community.

3. **To the woman he said, "I will surely multiply your pain in childbearing; in pain you shall bring forth children. Your desire shall be for your husband, and he shall rule over you." And to Adam he said, "Because you have listened to the voice of your wife and have eaten of the tree of which I commanded you, 'You shall not eat of it,' cursed is the ground because of you; in pain you shall eat of it all the days of your life; thorns**

and thistles it shall bring forth for you; and you shall eat the plants of the field. By the sweat of your face you shall eat bread, till you return to the ground, for out of it you were taken; for you are dust, and to dust you shall return." The man called his wife's name Eve, because she was the mother of all living. And the LORD God made for Adam and for his wife garments of skins and clothed them. Then the LORD God said, "Behold, the man has become like one of us in knowing good and evil. Now, lest he reach out his hand and take also of the tree of life and eat, and live forever—" therefore the LORD God sent him out from the garden of Eden to work the ground from which he was taken. (Genesis 3:16-23)

I've already stated that these are words which God speaks directly, first to Eve then to Adam. The Genesis text doesn't label this account as a wedding for the first couple. But I want to point out this passage has a structure liturgically parallel to a wedding. Picture the scene. Adam and Eve are standing before God. God first speaks to Eve, giving her his instructions or charge. God tells her she shall give birth to children and raise them with her husband. Then God speaks to Adam, giving him instructions. God tells Adam he shall work hard to support his wife and family.

In this story, Adam speaks the oath for both of them. Adam speaks to his new wife by giving her the new name, Eve, which defines her as mother, and by implication, he defines himself as father. This is a procreative marriage; and the first couple is accepting God's instruction by promising to be parents. Their job, at this initial stage of God's Creation, is to begin building the human population.

As this scene unfolds, the first couple doesn't exchange rings as symbols of their union. Instead, God makes clothes for them to wear as a symbol of their union. You might say God makes them wedding clothes. Finally, in good liturgical style, God tells the couple to go forth. God sends the couple out of the safety of Eden to struggle together to make their way through life's difficulties. Let me point out, that although Genesis doesn't label this passage as a wedding event, it has a similar structure and progression.

I suggest that when we see this similarity, we can begin to see that the Genesis story of Adam and Eve does not pretend to be the model for all future marriages. The verses which I'm describing as similar to a wedding liturgy, portray the first couple's relationship in terms familiar to both nomadic and hunter-gatherer cultures. The man was to work; the woman was to do childcare. Farming families follow a different pattern. Both men and women work full time. Men work the land; women manage the home and business (see Proverbs 31). But the irreducible heart of marriage throughout cultures is the commitment between two people before God to love each other and join their lives together for a lifetime. Here Adam and Eve's marriage is portrayed specifically in terms typical of nomadic and hunter-gatherer families.

4. Adam knew Eve his wife. (Genesis 4:1)

This is the Bible's first mention of human sex. It comes right after the passage I'm suggesting functions like the first couple's marriage service. And it concludes with the announcement that Eve has conceived and given birth to a son. In effect, Adam and Eve are married, then they give birth to their first child. As fits their role in launching human civilization, their marriage produces offspring.

I want to raise an important question here. Had there been sex between Adam and Eve in the Garden, before they sinned? We have to be careful asking a question like this. We don't want to try to force Scripture to answer questions which it doesn't intend to answer. But I suggest there are some conclusions we can eliminate and some we can safely propose. I believe we can propose that a non-procreative sexual relationship between Adam and Eve existed in the Garden. There's nothing specific I can say about this pre-Fall sexual relationship because Scripture tells us nothing. But Scripture also gives us good reason to eliminate the idea that human sexual relations are the result of the human fall into sin.

The church used to teach that sexual desire was the root of all sinful impulses. I suggest the church was right to move away from this way of thinking. I further suggest it is a faithful reading of Scripture, especially considering the enthusiastic description of human sexual feelings found in the Song of Solomon, to conclude human sexuality is a good thing, blessed by God. I suggest the meaning of Hebrews 13:3 is that God honors sexually faithful marriages and wants all people to honor sexually faithful marriages. If, as I'm suggesting, there was a non-procreative sexual relationship between Adam and Eve in the garden, it was certainly sexually faithful. And, if we eliminate the conclusion that the post-fall, procreative sexual relationship mentioned in Genesis 4:1 was the first sexual interaction between Adam and Eve, then the only conclusion left is that their sexual relationship began naturally during their days in Eden.

5. **"Also Ruth the Moabite, the widow of Mahlon, I have bought to be my wife . . . . You are witnesses this day." (Ruth 4:10)**

   So Boaz took Ruth, and she became his wife. And he went in to her, and the LORD gave her conception, and she bore a son. (Ruth 4:13)

In the book of Ruth, the marriage of Ruth and Boaz is described as a two part process. First Boaz takes Ruth as his wife, as stated in Ruth 4:10. Then the two have sexual relations and she bears a son, as stated in Ruth 4:13. Let me suggest that in Scripture, there is a direct correspondence between sexual intercourse and marriage. Interestingly, in the Ten Commandments, neither weddings or marriages are mentioned. Sexual faithfulness is mentioned. And respect for your neighbor's wife is mentioned. But the closest thing to a definition of marriage in the Moral Law is the command to be sexually faithful (Exodus 20:14). I suggest we want to look closely at the extent to which a faithful sexual relationship comprises and even defines marriage.

An earlier event in the book of Ruth, which can be interpreted sexually, takes place between Ruth and Boaz. Depending on how we understand this passage, it's possible that first Boaz and Ruth have sexual intercourse, then they officially marry. As the story of Ruth develops, Naomi, Ruth's mother-in-law, tells Ruth to go after Boaz to make him her husband. She directs Ruth to meet Boaz at night on the threshing floor. According to Naomi's plan, Ruth lay down next to Boaz and uncovered his feet, waking him up. Boaz then covered Ruth with the corner of his blanket. This has the metaphoric and idiomatic implication of a sexual act – an act that seals the couple's marriage. See:

> **After Boaz finished eating and drinking and was feeling happy, he went over and fell asleep near the pile of grain. Ruth slipped over quietly. She lifted the cover and lay down near his feet. In the middle of the night, Boaz suddenly woke up and was shocked to see a woman lying at his feet. "Who are you?" he asked. "Sir, I am Ruth," she answered, "and you are the relative who is supposed to take care of me. So spread the edge of your cover over me." (Ruth 3:7-9 CEV)**

Another biblical example where covering a woman with the corner or edge of a male's blanket is a symbolic or metaphorical sign of a sexual act which seals their marriage is in Ezekiel chapter 16. In Ezekiel, the husband is God and the wife is Israel. See:

> **When I (the LORD) passed by you again and saw you (Israel), behold, you were at the age for love, and I spread the corner of my garment over you and covered your nakedness; I made my vow to you and entered into a covenant with you, declares the Lord GOD, and you became mine. (Ezekiel 16:8.)**

I suggest the Ruth and Ezekiel passages both describe sexual intercourse as an act that seals the contract of marriage. But is there any other indication Scripture correlates sexual intercourse with marriage? I suggest there is.

6. **If a man meets a virgin who is not betrothed, and seizes her and lies with her, and they are found, then the man who lay with her shall give to the father of the young woman fifty shekels of silver, and she shall be his wife, because he has violated her. He may not divorce her all his days. (Deuteronomy 22:28-29)**

Deuteronomy chapter twenty two, is Jewish Judicial or civil Law, not Moral Law. But it adds another important indication that sexual intercourse is intrinsic to the sealing of marriage. Let's consider this passage then evaluate the overall relationship between sex and marriage in a Christian context.

In chapter twenty-two of Deuteronomy, several scenarios of improper sexual actions are described, and for each scenario a punishment is given. In verses 28 – 29, an unmarried, unattached man has sex with an unmarried, unattached woman. The consequence is neither severe nor fatal. The man has to pay the woman's father 50 silver shekels, which is half the fine for ruining the reputation of a virgin (Deuteronomy 22:19). The man must take the woman as his wife and may not divorce her. It is sometimes suggested this passage describes the consequences for rape. This is a possible interpretation. However, the preceding verses, 25 - 27, clearly describe rape. In the rape scenario, the man meets and overpowers a betrothed (officially engaged) woman out in the country where, if she yells, no one will hear her. The penalty for the man is death. My suggestion is that the verses under consideration, verses 28 – 29, describe something less serious than rape.

Rape is a predatory crime likely to go unreported because the rapist threatens his victim into silence. This passage assumes the sexual encounter becomes known. It may be the rapists in question are not particularly bright or careful, and plan their attacks where they can be easily observed. Or it might be the sex in verses 28-29 is consensual and is self-reported by the couple.

The possibility of consensual sex is not mentioned in this passage, at least in part, because human sex in the Hebrew world view is exclusively about the man's power and the man's choice. However, we just saw an example of a sexual overture from the book of Ruth where a sexual overture was initiated by a young woman that then led to marriage. Because of Ruth's example, we know a Hebrew woman of good character was not always sexually passive. A general knowledge of human nature would suggest this passage might well apply to sex desired by both the young man and the young woman. The text might well mean, if two young people want each other and can't wait to have sex, provision is made for them. They approach the girl's father and explain their situation. They give her father 50 shekels and are considered a married couple.

Whether this text describes rape, or a young couple's impetuous sexual tryst, the result is the same. The couple is to be married. A public marriage might better come before sexual relations; but if the sexual relations begin first, the couple becomes acceptable in the sight of God and their community by marrying each other. A marriage may begin with the man negotiating with the woman's father. But if sex occurs first, the couple's sexual congress is taken as an expression of marriage. The couple can satisfy God and society with a wedding that makes their marriage public.

Do Christians believe every couple who has sex should get married or that every couple who has sex is already married in God's sight? Neither is true. Deuteronomy chapter 22 is an example of Hebrew Judicial Law which we do not believe is intended to govern our lives today. This text is not Moral Law, which is contained exclusively in the Ten Commandments. However, it does describe an important aspect of human sexual experience. Sex can be a powerfully binding experience between two people. Clearly though, not every couple who has sexual intercourse intends to begin a marriage. They may intend a onetime experience or a causal relationship with an "on again off again" sexual component.

So, how do we describe the overall relationship between sex and marriage in a Christian context? I suggest sex only signifies and seals a marriage when two people have already pledged before God to give themselves to each other for a lifetime. A Christian Marriage may begin with a church wedding. However, if sexual relations begin first, a Christian couple can satisfy moral law, and society's expectations, with a church wedding through which they receive the public welcome of the Christian faith community.

7. You shall not commit adultery. (Exodus 20:14)

You shall not covet your neighbor's house; you shall not covet your neighbor's wife, or his male servant, or his female servant, or his ox, or his donkey, or anything that is your neighbor's. (Exodus 20:17)

God's law recognizes that human sexual interaction can be trivial, casual, and even an expression of power abuse. Sex can be devalued into being no more than a mutual masturbation in which two people physically pleasure each other. I suggest this is what the Bible calls lust. It takes place when one or both people use the other as object of sexual pleasure. But God's moral law calls God's people to a higher way of behaving sexually. I suggest God's moral law gives us two sexual commands. 1) Do not commit adultery by being sexually unfaithful. 2) Do not lust by desiring to take any person as a sexual object you can own and use for your sexual pleasure.

You'll notice the Ten Commandments are expressed as negatives. As *what not to do.* The Christian interpretive tradition tries to explain the Commandments as positive commands. What might be the positive way to express, "Do not be sexually unfaithful?" I suggest a positive restatement might be: Love your marriage partner with a faithful love like God's faithful love for his people and Christ's faithful love for the church. What might be the positive way to restate, "Do not desire to take any person as a sexual object you can own and use for your sexual pleasure?" I suggest we might say we are to treasure the holiness and sacredness of our sexual partner. We are to elevate our sexuality into the ecstatic physical, emotional, and spiritual union of two people.

8. **For your Maker is your husband, the LORD of hosts is his name; and the Holy One of Israel is your Redeemer, the God of the whole earth he is called. For the LORD has called you like a wife deserted and grieved in spirit, like a wife of youth when she is cast off, says your God. For a brief moment I deserted you, but with great compassion I will gather you. (Isaiah 54:5-7)**

   Husbands, love your wives, as Christ loved the church and gave himself up for her. "Therefore a man shall leave his father and mother and hold fast to his wife, and the two shall become one flesh." This mystery is profound, and I am saying that it refers to Christ and the church. (Ephesians 5:25, 31-32)

In both the Old and New Testaments, God's relationship with his people is compared to married love. Life has many experiences besides marriage through which we can learn the essential lessons of love. Singleness is where we all begin life. Singleness is where many live their whole adult lives. Singleness is where couples live either after divorce or after the death of a partner. But I suggest the frequent scriptural comparison of God's relationship with his people to married love indicates that the blessings of Christian Marriage are an important part of God's plan for human life. I suggest, at its best, Christian Marriage is a school where Christian people can learn to develop and exhibit God's kind of faithful love for each other.

9. **And the two shall become one flesh. (Ephesians 5:31)**

   "I (Jesus) do not ask for these (disciples) only, but also for those who will believe in me through their word, that they may all be one, just as you, Father, are in me, and I in you, that they also may be in us, so that the world may believe that you have sent me." (John 17:20-21)

In a previous letter, we talked about Paul's Christian reinterpretation of marriage in Ephesians chapter five. In the Old Covenant of Creation, marriage had been primarily understood as procreative relationship. In Christ's New Covenant of the New Creation, marriage is now understood as a faithful and self-sacrificial love relationship characterized by oneness and equality.

Christian oneness in Christ is a fundamental New Testament theme. Jesus mentions it in John 17 when he prays for his disciples. Paul also mentions it frequently in his epistles. And it is around this theme of oneness that Paul reinterprets Christian Marriage. Christian Marriage is to embody the love and unity through which the world can see Christ's love at work and come to believe in God's goodness.

10. **And we all, with unveiled face, beholding the glory of the Lord, are being transformed into the same image from one degree of glory to another. For this comes from the Lord who is the Spirit. (2 Corinthians 3:18)**

    Beloved, let us love one another, for love is from God, and whoever loves has been born of God and knows God. So we have come to know and to believe the love that God has for us. God is love, and whoever abides in love abides in God, and God abides in him. (1 John 4:7, and 16)

    The LORD passed before him (Moses) and proclaimed, "The LORD, the LORD, a God merciful and gracious, slow to anger, and abounding in steadfast love and faithfulness." (Exodus 34:6)

As we come to the end of our biblical definition of Christian Marriage, I will summarize these last four verses succinctly. God's purpose for Christian Marriage is not separate from God's purpose in every Christian's life. II Corinthians 3:18 states the purpose of God's Spirit in every Christian's life is transforming us, one step at a time, into sharing the glory of God's character. In I John 4:7 and 16, God's character is described as love; and God's desire for us is stated as to love each other with a love like God's. Exodus 34:6 makes it clear that, "God is love," isn't just a New Testament idea. In this pivotal scene, God describes himself to Moses as, "merciful and gracious, slow to anger, and abounding in steadfast love and faithfulness." It is this faithful love that God wants to teach Christians to express whether as singles or as married couples. Experiencing and living out this love fulfills a Christian's humanity, which is our inner Imago Dei, our inner God likeness; and it blesses every human culture it touches.

This brings us to the end of our discussion of *The Discipline of Family Love*. The next chapters will be written by you, the Christian couples who are reading these words. These chapters will be written, not in words on paper, but in your loving actions as married couples.

Warmly in Christ,

$\int teve$

The Rev. Steve R. Wigall, Th.M., Th.D.

Lawrence, Massachusetts

———————————

How irreverent are the stiff and stuffy!
Who is less Godly than those who reject joy and laughter?
Who dishonors the Creator more than those who refuse to be earthy?
How wild and beautiful our God – who is in love with all creation
and every person!
Who can keep God's love from healing human hearts with celestial
laughter and joy?

LESSON SIX

DISCUSSION QUESTIONS

Class Opening

(Leader) Gracious God, (pray in unison) **teach us to love each other as a couple with a Christ-like love. Teach us to know each other as Christ knows us. Teach us to take joy in each other as Christ takes joy in us.**

When love gets hard, let us be patient with each other as you are patient. Let us strive to be understanding as you understand. Let us be faithful to each other as you are faithful.

Grant that through our shared successes and failures, through our shared happiness and sorrow, we might find lasting joy in the lessons of love which you teach us. We pray in the name of Jesus Christ, who shows us your love, calls us to love, and empowers us with your love. Amen

The Discipline of Family Love: 10 (cont.)

10 (cont.) Strive to Build a Lasting Love Relationship

(6)   Create an enduring bond of trust and honesty.

Questions to discuss:

Questions about trust

1. What questions do you have from the Couple's Pamphlet or from the Couple's Letter(s)? Ask the couple or couples, "Is there homework from our last session? Are there questions that have come to

your mind since we last met or talked?" Share homework.

2. What moves you to trust your partner? What gets in the way of trust?

3. Since you've known each other, what has happened to put stress on your trust in each other? How did you restore the trust between you?

Questions about confession

4. Do you believe lashing out in anger a) clears the air or b) makes it harder for your partner to listen to you?

5. When you explain your hurt feelings, you believe you should a) explain clearly why your hurt is your partner's fault so they cannot escape their responsibility, or b) risk honestly telling your partner how you feel – without placing blame?

6. Is it better to a) use all the energy and bravery which anger can give you to nail your partner to the wall, or b) use the energy of your anger to risk telling the person who has hurt you how wounded you feel?

7. The best approach is to a) say you're sorry as fast as you can to get the argument out of the way, or b) after you have listened with understanding and empathy, and re-established trust, then say you are sorry.

Questions about profession

8. "Profession" means a) sharing Christ's Good News with your partner, or b) regularly sharing your deepest values and most important convictions with your partner?

9. A marriage relationship survives long term a) because the couple has learned to enjoy sharing "small talk," or b) because they've learned to keep on sharing and discussing their personal beliefs,

or c) both?

10. Daily life is easier a) when you can interject profound issues to discuss, or b) when you can honestly share your thoughts and feelings in reaction to the events of the day?

Concluding QUESTIONS and ANSWERS about Christian Marriage

Q.   How does a couple enter into Christian Marriage?

A.   Christian Marriage begins when two people promise before God to love each other exclusively for as long as they live and express their commitment through sexual union. Christian Marriage is consecrated when the church celebrates the joining of these two lives through a Christian wedding which publicly recognizes their place as a married couple within the Christian faith community.

Questions to discuss:

11. What advantage, if any, is there for a couple who makes a life-long commitment to be marriage partners before beginning a sexual relationship?

12. What is the distinction between a Christian Marriage and a Christian Wedding?

13. Discuss the following statement. (It is another way of answering the question is above, "How does a couple enter into Christian Marriage?") A Christian Marriage may begin with a Christian Wedding for which the couple makes the proper arrangements with both families and the church. However, if sexual relations begin first, the couple's sexual congress is taken to be an expression of their marriage in the sight of God. The couple can then satisfy moral "propriety" and society's expectations by making arrangements for a Christian Wedding, through which they make their marriage public and receive the welcome and blessing of the Christian Faith community.

Q. What is the essence of Christian Marriage?

A. The essential and defining characteristic of Christian Marriage is a commitment between two people to love each other faithfully for a lifetime.

Q. What is the difference between Christian Marriage and civil marriage?

A. Christian Marriage is the spiritual union of two people which is recognized by God and validated by the Christian Church. Civil marriage is a legal partnership between two people which meets the requirements for marriage according to the laws of the state in which the couple resides.

Q. Who may receive Christian Marriage?

A. The many blessings of Christian Marriage belong to any couple who shows they want those blessings by willingly accepting all The Disciplines of Family Love.

Q. What is the purpose of Christian Marriage?

A. The blessings of Christian Marriage are an essential part of God's plan for human life. At its best, Christian Marriage:

  ☐ Embodies the characteristics of God's love,

  ☐ Is a means through which God transforms a couple into Christ-likeness, and

  ☐ Offers the promise of human fulfillment to a couple and their community.

(Genesis 1:26-28, Exodus 34:6, 1 John 4:16, 2 Corinthians 3:18)

SECTION 2

A DISCUSSION GUIDE FOR CLERGY FOR THE COUPLE'S PAMPHLET

Preparing for Christian Marriage

INTRODUCTION TO THE DISCUSSION GUIDE FOR CLERGY

This Guide for Clergy is Section 2 of *An Inclusive Handbook for Straight and LGBTQ Couples Seeking a Joyful Marriage.* Section 1 begins with the text of a pamphlet for couples seeking Christian Marriage entitled, *Preparing for Christian Marriage.* Section 1 includes six personal letters written to the participating couples explicating Christian Marriage and six discussion sheets, one to accompany each letter or lesson. Section 3 is a theological position paper which explains the biblical basis for civil Marriage Equality and Christian Marriage inclusivity from the viewpoint of Reformed

Theology, written for the use of pastors, counselors, and Christian educators. Here in Section 2, you will find a point-by-point Discussion Guide for Clergy, with commentary on the text of *Preparing for Christian Marriage: Couple's Pamphlet,* which you will be able to use for teaching a class, leading a discussion, or counseling couples using the couple's pamphlet.

This Guide for Clergy discusses a number of supportive Scripture passages which make it clear that Scripture does more than define what marriage is; it describes the qualities that make marriage a vital (although not essential) part of the Christian life. This Guide pays special attention to the scriptural basis for *The Discipline of Family Love* which is described in the couple's pamphlet. It follows the interpretative guidance of the Reformed confessions by not adding moral parameters to marriage beyond those contained in the Ten Commandments. But it also pays attention to scriptural texts and themes which qualify as marital beatitudes or indicators of marital happiness. It should not be a surprise the Old Testament Wisdom literature and the New Testament epistles both have passages of beatitude or guidance which apply to marriage.

In the body of this Guide for Clergy, the text of the couple's pamphlet is reproduced, phrase by phrase. Its text is set out in **bold**. Following each statement from the couple's pamphlet, there will be a section marked, <u>Questions to discuss with the couple</u>, which lists discussion questions and discussion starters which pastors, counselors, and Christian educators may use for teaching and counselling couples. When appropriate, there is also a section marked <u>For the Pastor / Counselor</u>. This section provides scriptural and confessional background for pastors, counselors, and Christian educators who are working with couples desiring Christian Marriage. The six personal letters to couples in Section 1 go over much of the same background material – just deeply enough to get the couples thinking about the subject matter of each lesson and to put them in a good position to ask questions and engage in discussion led by you, their pastor, counselor, or Christian educator. The couples will read the appropriate letter(s) and corresponding discussion sheet(s) before each session or lesson they have with you. You'll want to read these letters, too, so you can discuss them and answer questions about them with the couple(s) you are guiding through this process.

Before the first session

Make sure each couple knows and has agreed to the dates and times set aside for the counseling or class sessions. Decide with the couple or couples whether there will be three or six sessions. Before the agreed-upon beginning date, provide each couple, or better yet each individual, with a copy of the couple's pamphlet, a set of the six letters, and the six discussion sheets – all are in Section 1 of the text. Because each participant will need their own discussion pages for use during class sessions, it would be ideal for each participant to have their own book. Encourage couples, whenever possible, to secure two copies of the book, one for each of them to use. Have them read the text of the pamphlet, *Preparing for Christian Marriage*, and write down any questions or comments that occur to them as they read. Instruct them to also read the letter or letters that introduce the lesson they are studying that week. Have them underline sentences they want to discuss further and note in the margins any questions they have. Let them know you will encourage their questions during your sessions with them. Remind the couple(s) at the beginning of each session that their questions and comments are welcome.

Before each session

Direct the couple to skim through the discussion pages for each week's session. They'll find their copy of the discussion pages in their class text. Take time yourself to read through the 12 to 18 discussion questions and discussion starters for the session. Then, in the copy from which you are teaching, in Section 2 of the text, mark one-third to one-half of the questions and discussion starters for your use during the upcoming session. Note for each session, there will be more questions on the discussion pages than you will be able to talk about during that session. For each session, the questions are grouped topically. Try to use at least one or two questions from each of the topical groups; but don't worry about covering every question. Your couples can use the questions not discussed in class for at-home discussion between themselves.

Beginning each session

Begin each session with a prayer for couples. You might copy and distribute to the participating couples a prayer such as this one, found also in the discussion pages. You could also make sure each couple or each individual has a copy of the book to use during class discussions, so they can more easily follow the discussion questions, and pray along with this opening prayer:

> (Leader) Gracious God, (pray in unison) **teach us to love each other as a couple with a Christ-like love. Teach us to know each other as Christ knows us. Teach us to take joy in each other as Christ takes joy in us.**
>
> **When love gets hard, let us be patient with each other as you are patient. Let us strive to be understanding as you understand. Let us be faithful to each other as you are faithful.**
>
> **Grant that through our shared successes and failures, through our shared happiness and sorrow, we might find lasting joy in the lessons of love which you teach us. We pray in the name of Jesus Christ, who shows us your love, calls us to love, and empowers us with your love. Amen**

If you are leading a discussion group, or teaching a class, plan to follow the opening prayer with an icebreaker question. The question should be both personal and silly. Personal, to promote discussion; and silly, to break down barriers and make it easier to speak up in the group. People are often willing to be as serious in their sharing as they have first been silly, and laughed together about it. I suggest icebreaker questions such as:

1. What was your favorite candy bar when you were a child? Why did you like it?

2. Briefly describe your childhood bedroom.

3. If you had to be a superhero for a week, which superhero would you like to be, and why?

4. If you could go on a vacation to an exotic or special place, with money as no object, where would you like to go? What would you like to do there?

5. What is your favorite kind of weather, and why?

6. Tell us one of your earliest school memories.

Discuss the Session Questions

Ask the couple or couples, "Is there homework from our last session? Have questions come to your mind since we last met or talked, especially from the reading?" Share homework. Discuss any questions.

Spend the bulk of the session discussing the questions on the discussion page which you, as the pastor, counselor, or group teacher, have chosen. Read together the pamphlet text, which is printed in bold, both on the discussion pages, and in the Discussion Guide for Clergy. Don't try to get through all the questions. Couples can work on unanswered questions at home together during the week.

End on time.

Conclude each group session or class by praying in unison The Lord's Prayer. Instead, you may choose to conclude private counseling sessions with a prayer for the couple.

Remember: the time prior to marriage is a delightful one in the life of couples. They are full of questions and yet are imbued with the confidence of love. It is a time when many couples are open to being ministered to, maybe for the first time in their adult lives. This is true whether it is the couple's first marriage or a re-marriage. The prospect of marriage has a way of throwing all of us off balance. Be encouraging; and let the couple(s) know you are enjoying working with them. This is an important part of making this a positive experience for you and for them.

A Discussion Guide for Clergy and Commentary on the Couple's Pamphlet for Couples Desiring Christian Marriage Entitled
Preparing for Christian Marriage
Expanding on the Biblical and Confessional Basis for
The Discipline of Family Love

Before the First Session

This commentary is designed to provide more background material, discussion questions, and discussion starters than a pastor, counselor, or Christian educator can use. There should be more than enough material for the six suggested sessions and considerably more than enough for three sessions. Decide with your couple or couples whether you will hold six or three sessions. You can then tailor the lessons to the needs of your couple(s). Before beginning each lesson, read the Personal Couple Letter or Letters the couples are reading for that Lesson. Note points from the letters you'd like to expand on. Then mark for use one-third to one-half of the 12 to 18 questions on each session's discussion pages. How many of the discussion questions you, as a leader, may need to use will depend on the number and length of the sessions and on how talkative your class or couple turns out to be. You and the couple(s) will want to agree how long each session will last. 60 minutes might be a minimum. 90 minutes might be optimal. 120 minutes or two hours might be a maximum, but perhaps useful for a shorter three session program.

The First Session

After an opening prayer and icebreaker, begin the first class, discussion group, or counseling series with the questions marked, Class Overview. The following is an outline for both 3 and 6 sessions which you can share with the participating couple(s).

Lesson One, or, Lessons One and Two

    1. A Christian Marriage creates FAMILY.

    2. A Christian Marriage teaches LOVE.

    A Christian Marriage teaches LIFE IN COMMUNITY

Lesson Two, or, Lessons Three and Four

    3. *The Discipline of Family Love*: I – V

    4. *The Discipline of Family Love*: VI – IX

Lesson Three, or, Lessons Five and Six

    5. *The Discipline of Family Love*: X

    6. *The Discipline of Family Love*: X (cont.)

    Summary and Concluding Questions

After surveying the course material, ask the participating couple(s) for any initial, general questions about Christian Marriage which they may have. Remember, you will have insured each participant has a class text, which includes the couple's pamphlet and appropriate couple letter(s), prior to this first meeting. This assures each person will have the material they need to participate in the discussion. Answer and discuss the couple's initial questions then begin directly with the discussion questions and discussion starters from Lesson One: "A Christian Marriage creates FAMILY." Read together the pamphlet text which is printed in bold in both the discussion pages and in the Discussion Guide for Clergy. Then discuss the questions you've chosen. Share background material only when you think it is necessary to enable discussion.

LESSON ONE

Class Opening

> (Leader) Gracious God, (pray in unison) **teach us to love each other as a couple with a Christ-like love. Teach us to know each other as Christ knows us. Teach us to take joy in each other as Christ takes joy in us.**
>
> **When love gets hard, let us be patient with each other as you are patient. Let us strive to be understanding as you understand. Let us be faithful to each other as you are faithful.**
>
> **Grant that through our shared successes and failures, through our shared happiness and sorrow, we might find lasting joy in the lessons of love which you teach us. We pray in the name of Jesus Christ, who shows us your love, calls us to love, and empowers us with your love. Amen**

1)   Ask the icebreaker question. (See the Guide for Clergy introduction.)

2)   Begin with the discussion questions you've chosen for this session.

You Are Thinking About Christian Marriage . . .

". . . Yes, we are. We love each other and want to spend our lives together. Isn't that what Christian Marriage *is all about*?"

It is. Christian Marriage is a faithful, loving relationship between two people who commit to being life partners. That *is* what *it's all about* – that . . . and *so much more*.

Class Overview

<u>Questions to discuss with the couple</u>:

1. What questions do you have from the Couple's Pamphlet or from the Couple's Letter(s)? Discuss any questions.

2. How do you feel about the following definition? Christian Marriage can be defined as a faithful, loving relationship between two people who commit to being life partners.

3. What might distinguish Christian Marriage from civil marriage? Respond to the following three affirmations. (We will be discussing them further during this study.):

   a. A Christian Marriage creates FAMILY.

   b. A Christian Marriage teaches LOVE.

   c. A Christian Marriage teaches LIFE IN COMMUNITY.

Christian Marriage *Is All About* . . . Family.

Or: A Christian Marriage creates FAMILY.

Christian Marriage is a good thing. It makes families; and family is both one of God's best blessings and most difficult disciplines. Accepting Christian Marriage means accepting the blessing and *The Discipline of Family Love.*

<u>For the Pastor / Counselor</u>:

Married love is referred to in these documents as: *The Discipline of Family Love*. Notice that no one section of Scripture is dedicated to defining the qualities of *The Discipline of Family Love*. But the subject of love, and married love in particular, is discussed in many places in both the Old and New Testaments. Two of the ten moral laws (the Ten Commandments) apply directly to *The Discipline of Family Love*. Many verses within the scriptural books of Wisdom describe important components of *The Discipline of Family Love*. Many sections of the New Testament letters (epistles) give good relationship advice which applies to *The Discipline of Family Love*. Some sections of the epistles directly explain *The Discipline of Family Love* as it pertains to married couples. And throughout the Scriptures, God's actions towards God's people are held up as an example of the passionate and reconciling love which informs *The Discipline of Family Love*.

Questions to discuss with the couple:

4. Do you agree with the following observation? In romantic relationships, we are commonly attracted to individuals different enough from us to fascinate us, disappoint us, get under our skin, and anger us.

5. Celebrating and enjoying your partner's similarities and differences is one of love's greatest blessings. Learning with a partner to work through your anger and your emotional wounds is one of love's greatest difficulties. How do you feel about taking on both love's blessings and difficulties?

6. Respond to the following observation. When we let someone close enough to us to love us, we let them close enough to both bless us and hurt us.

Christians strongly believe in the importance of family. Family relationships give shape, strength, and purpose to the lives of children as they grow towards maturity. In family relationships, children learn to love, to think of others, and to make a difference for good in the world. Family relationships are part of *The Discipline of Family Love*.

<u>For the Pastor / Counselor</u>:

All children need to be treated with respect and gently taught in the ways of love. However, neither society nor church can mandate every family and every community organization responsible for child care to give respectful and loving nurture. What can society do? It can criminalize all violence against children. It could also legally enshrine the value the human rights of children, as it is summarized, for example, in such declarations as, The Convention of the Rights of the Child, UNICEF (1989, 1990, 1995, & 2002). Society can further protect the rights of children the way it *informally* (i.e. extra-legally) protects other civil rights.

Society could mobilize its most powerful instrument for educating its citizens, the public school and public university systems, requiring them to teach students the value of respect for all people. These systems could also be required to teach the value of all families as important places where children are to be safely nurtured and where both children and adults can find their need for love met. Schools and colleges could also involve students in group participation exercises, group learning experiences, and community service projects through which they could learn the important family values of cooperation, teamwork, and community concern.

What can the church do? The church exercises its power through teaching and persuasion. It can combine biblical wisdom with the best psychological insights of the day in order to teach its families, through sermons, classes, and seminars, how to respect and nurture family members of all ages. The church's persuasive power functions *informally*, through its welcome at worship, at the communion table, and at its activities. The church exercises its persuasive power *formally* through its organizational rules which prescribe who can be a member, and who can be a leader. The church needs the social grace to warmly accept both heterosexual and same-sex couples into its fellowship, whether they are dating or engaged, or married. The church also needs to ensure its official organizational rules welcome into membership all people who are interested in accepting its beliefs and values, and accept qualified members as leaders – regardless of race, gender, age, or sexual orientation.

<u>Questions to discuss with the couple</u>:

7. It is important for couples seeking marriage to think about the values their new family will stand for. Each individual make a list of no more than five values you'd like your new family to uphold. Share and compare your lists.

8. Respond to the statement: Christian families will want to model for and impart to their children the citizenship values of co-operation, teamwork, respect for each person's dignity, a commitment to uphold human rights (and children's rights), and community service.

9. Respond to the statement: Christian families will want to model for and impart to their children the Christian value of an open acceptance of all persons, especially Christian persons – regardless of race, gender, age, or sexual orientation. (See Galatians 6:10)

10. What do you think might be the hardest part of developing the social grace within your family of warmly accepting both heterosexual and same-sex couples and families in your home and in your church fellowship?

When we mature as individuals, we leave our fathers and mothers and may seek a life partner with whom we can join to create families of our own. In these new families, we hope to find and share

the companionship and support which all people need. Joining with a life partner is also part of *The Discipline of Family Love.*

For the Pastor / Counselor:

The descriptions of marriage, in Genesis 2 and Ephesians 5, both contain this developmental observation that as a man (and a woman) grow toward maturity, they leave their parent's home, and become independent from them by seeking and taking a life-mate. One way we can be sure these descriptions of marriage are not commands that apply to all people or all marriages is that there is no support within Scripture, or outside of it within Hebrew or Christian tradition, for *requiring* all people to leave their parent's homes as they grow up. Neither is there scriptural support for *requiring* all people to marry. This is further indication both the Genesis and the Ephesians passages regarding marriage are descriptive observations, not mandates.

Questions to discuss with the couple:

11. Courtship is an important part of the human search for family love. The second part of this search involves building family relationships through which our need for love can be met. At this point in your courtship, how are the two of you doing at building family (in-law) relationships?

12. You are starting a new family, which will be separate (distinct, not necessarily geographically distant) from your two families of origin. How are you doing as a couple in establishing emotional distance from your families of origin? How are you doing as individuals at this task?

13. Society needs as many of its citizens as possible to become couples by successfully courting and marrying each other, and going on from there, to form strong and loving families. How have you experienced social support during your courtship? How have you experienced interference?

14. Courtship is a difficult and highly emotional time. It can be both exhilarating and defeating, empowering and heart breaking. What has been difficult about your courtship? What has been the best part?

    For the Pastor / Counselor:

    American society tends to find its heterosexual couples endearing and supports them in their community with dances, at restaurants with the best tables, on Valentine's Day with the best flower arrangements, and as they walk down the street hand in hand with the smiles of strangers. Same-sex couples are not encouraged to court in the same way. In many places, same-sex couples are neither favored nor welcomed. Scowls and frowns instead of warm smiles more often meet them when they walk hand in hand. The number of social venues that encourage and nurture same-sex romantic relationships is very small. Society has an interest in ensuring all same-sex couples, (dating, engaged, and married) are not excluded from romantic venues.

15. Homework: Suggest couples purchase a small notebook and label it, "Family Goals." Suggest each couple take the next week to record in the notebook the values they want their family to stand for and pass on to children, if they have children. Announce couples will be invited to share their values lists at your next meeting. Suggest that couples repeat this exercise between themselves on an annual basis.

LESSON TWO

Class Opening

> (Leader) Gracious God, (pray in unison) **teach us to love each other as a couple with a Christ-like love. Teach us to know each other as Christ knows us. Teach us to take joy in each other as Christ takes joy in us.**
>
> **When love gets hard, let us be patient with each other as you are patient. Let us strive to be understanding as you understand. Let us be faithful to each other as you are faithful.**
>
> **Grant through our shared successes and failures, through our shared happiness and sorrow, we might find lasting joy in the lessons of love which you teach us. We pray in the name of Jesus Christ, who shows us your love, calls us to love, and empowers us with your love. Amen**

1) Ask the icebreaker question. (See the Guide for Clergy introduction.)

2) Begin with the discussion questions you've chosen for this session.

Christian Marriage *Is All About* . . . Learning to Love

Or: A Christian Marriage teaches LOVE.

***The Discipline of Family Love* is both joyous and vexing because it involves us in relationships that confront us with life's greatest blessings and life's greatest difficulties. God intends for us to grow in our ability to love through being enriched by the blessings of family love and strengthened by its difficulties.**

136

Questions to discuss with the couple:

1. What questions do you have from the Couple's Pamphlet or from the Couple's Letter(s)? Ask the couple or couples, "Is there homework from our last session? Are there questions that have come to your mind since we last met or talked?" Share homework.

2. To what degree are you getting married because of the pressure of family and friends? Has that pressure been a helpful motivator or an unhelpful interference?

3. Would adult, single Christians be right to feel deprived or feel like social outsiders? If you do not get married, or, if your marriage partner dies, would you face the end of a valuable life, or an end to experiencing love? Why or why not?

4. Do you believe singleness is a status God honors and blesses? How can the meaning and the richness of love be experienced by unmarried persons?

5. Would it change your life to believe coital sex belongs exclusively in faithful marriage relationships? If so, how?

Starting a new family by marrying a life partner is not the only way to learn the lessons of love. Singleness is also a normal part of human life. All married people begin life by being single and may become single again if their marriage ends. Many people are single for a lifetime. Fortunately, God can bring all the blessing and discipline of love into the lives of people who find themselves single or who choose to remain single.

Questions to discuss with the couple:

6. Seeking Christian Marriage is seeking a good thing. Can you see signs God has led you to want to create a family of your own? Can you see signs God has led you to find that special

marriage partner with whom to create it? What signs have you seen?

7. Approach Christian Marriage with every hope of happiness and joy; but realize, even with God's blessing your marriage will not achieve unbroken bliss. What skills do you bring to your marriage for coping with its inevitable disappointments?

8. Couples seeking Christian Marriage need to be realistic about how difficult it will be to keep growing in the love for their chosen partner for a lifetime. What strategies do you bring to your marriage for keeping love alive?

9. Take stock, as best you can, of your readiness to meet the demands of love throughout all of life's stages and crises. As Jesus said, a builder will take stock of his supplies before he begins to build a tower; and before a king goes to war, he will count the size of his army and the sufficiency of his ammunition (Luke 14:28–33).

For which of you, desiring to build a tower, does not first sit down and count the cost, whether he has enough to complete it? Otherwise, when he has laid a foundation and is not able to finish, all who see it begin to mock him, saying, 'This man began to build and was not able to finish.' Or what king, going out to encounter another king in war, will not sit down first and deliberate whether he is able with ten thousand to meet him who comes against him with twenty thousand? And if not, while the other is yet a great way off, he sends a delegation and asks for terms of peace. So therefore, anyone of you who does not renounce all that he has cannot be my disciple.

Homework: To facilitate taking stock, make a list of the 3 to 5 hardest challenges you anticipate facing together in your married life. Share and discuss each other's lists. Decide and mark how tough each life challenge might be on a scale of 1 to 10, with 1 being easiest and 10 being hardest.

However, God *commonly* brings the discipline of love into human life through marriage and family. God even encourages people to look for a life partner whom they can marry and work with to create a new family. Christian Marriage is a good thing; but it offers neither a magic ticket to human happiness nor guarantees the new family a couple creates will be perfectly loving.

Questions to discuss with the couple:

10. The love that brings two people together in marriage is strong and creates the feeling within the couple, together they can do anything. What experiences have you had that shake your confidence in each other? At this point in time, how would you describe the strengths you see in your partner that give you confidence in him or her?

11. At the outset of marriage, it is important for Christian couples to recognize, because of their human weakness and brokenness, they will need God to be a third partner in their marriage. What signs have you seen you need God in your relationship?

12. How have you included God in your courtship? What specific activities can you as a couple do to make God an active part of your marriage?

Christians believe sin permeates the world and damages the human ability to form relationships – including family relationships. Consequently, accepting Christian Marriage means accepting that learning *The Discipline of Family Love* will be an ongoing and sometimes uphill, lifetime struggle.

For the Pastor / Counselor:

The consequences of the ubiquitous nature of sin are spelled out in detail in the "Study Paper." In brief, the Reformed doctrine of sin is an integral part of the doctrine of Grace. Sin

139

touches every part of each person's life. Even our best actions and most valuable talents are infected with sin. As a consequence, we cannot look down at another human as though we were better or as though they are in any way less worthy than ourselves. In this context, the doctrine of sin helps us face, without feeling guilt or shame, the brokenness within us that makes love an uphill struggle.

Questions to discuss with the couple:

13. When you look back at the marriage, or lack of marriage, of your childhood caregiver(s) and your early family life, you will see imperfections and even failures. What aspects of these marriages and formative families do you admire?

14. Accepting the failures in our family of origin can make it easier to accept our own failures to love perfectly. What 2 or 3 aspects of your family of origin do you have trouble accepting?

Christian Marriage *Is All About* . . . Living in Community.

Or: A Christian Marriage teaches LIFE IN COMMUNITY.

The presence of sin in the world means no one comes to Christian Marriage with a perfect experience of family love. It also means married couples can expect that creating a loving family will require a lifetime of work.

Consequently, every Christian family needs the support of the Christian faith community to help it handle *The Discipline of Family Love*. As all Christian people are welcome at Christ's communion table and none are to be excluded; so all Christian families are welcome in the supportive communion of Christ's church and none are to be excluded.

When we accept Christian Marriage, we will be called to reach out to and support the other families in the church community. In

return, we should expect the welcome of church families and be prepared to receive their support.

<u>For the Pastor / Counselor</u>:

Pastors need to counter the belief that "normal" Christian families will never need help or support from other families within the Christian community. The Christian poet, John Donne, wrote: "no man is an island;" but it is also true that *no couple is an island*. For so many reasons, every Christian family has a stake in the success and strength of the other families in their faith community. The Apostle Paul described every individual Christian as an interdependent part of the Body of Christ; but it is also true that every Christian family is an interdependent part of the Christian family. Every Christian family needs the gifts and strengths the Body of Christ can give, and the Body of Christ needs every family's gifts and strengths.

As the Christian church adjusts to the justice and rightness of Marriage Equality, one of its clear growing points will be to increasingly accept and incorporate same-sex couples and families with same-sex in-laws into its fellowship. As Marriage Equality and Marriage inclusivity become more accepted, it will mean heterosexual couples and families will increasingly find natural opportunities to develop friendships with same-sex couples and families with same-sex in-laws. Christian pastors will need to find ways to support this social change through their teaching and preaching ministries.

<u>Questions to discuss with the couple</u>:

15. To meet the challenges of family love, a Christian couple will need the strength and support of their church family. What hesitations do you have about asking for and accepting help from the church community?

16. A healthy marriage cannot exist in isolation. What might be hard about cultivating and accepting the friendship and encouragement of other loving Christian families?

17. The commitment of Christian Marriage is not only between (1) the two of you. It is also between (2) yourselves and God, and between (3) yourselves and the church community. How you feel about entering into this "three way" marriage commitment?

18. What strategies might you use for developing the kind of trusting relationships with other Christian couples that would allow for mutual support? What kind of activities do you think help create trust between couples?

19. Building a supportive network for your marriage will involve cultivating the grace of hospitality. How do you feel about using your home to extend friendship, table fellowship when possible, and help when needed, to other Christian couples within your faith community? Are you more temperamentally inclined to want your home to be an emotional refuge or to be a social center? How would each of you balance these two goals? (It is likely each of you will prefer a different balance.)

LESSON THREE

Class Opening

> (Leader) Gracious God, (pray in unison) **teach us to love each other as a couple with a Christ-like love. Teach us to know each other as Christ knows us. Teach us to take joy in each other as Christ takes joy in us.**
>
> **When love gets hard, let us be patient with each other as you are patient. Let us strive to be understanding as you understand. Let us be faithful to each other as you are faithful.**
>
> **Grant that through our shared successes and failures, through our shared happiness and sorrow, we might find lasting joy in the lessons of love which you teach us. We pray in the name of Jesus Christ, who shows us your love, calls us to love, and empowers us with your love. Amen**

1) Ask the icebreaker question. (See the Guide for Clergy introduction.)

2) Begin with the discussion questions you've chosen for this session.

The Discipline of Family Love: 1 - 5

Clearly, Christian Marriage is *so much more* than a relationship between two people who love each other and want to spend their lives together. But, exactly what does the *so much more* of Christian Marriage ask couples to *do*?

Christian Marriage asks couples to accept *The Discipline of Family Love*. For couples, this means taking the following actions and living by the following values, all of which find their basis in the

143

teaching of Scripture.

1. Be faithful to the one you love.

Do not betray the one you love by being sexually unfaithful to them.

(Exodus 20:14)

Questions to discuss with the couple:

1. What questions do you have from the Couple's Pamphlet or from the Couple's Letter(s)? Ask the couple or couples, "Is there homework from our last session? Are there questions that have come to your mind since we last met or talked?" Share homework.

2. Exodus 20:14 (above), is the first and most important moral commandment that applies to marriage. How does American culture help strengthen marriage and make faithfulness easier? How does American culture undermine marriage and make faithfulness harder?

3. The *Christian* meaning of this commandment is marriage requires a couple to commit before God and the Christian community to enter a lifelong sexually faithful relationship. How do you feel about the essential moral foundation of marriage being sexual faithfulness? Is this too strict a standard? Why or why not?

2. Do not "lust after" the one you love.

This means: do not violate the one you love by sexually objectifying or using them.

(Matthew 5:28; James 1:14; Exodus 20:17)

Questions to discuss with the couple:

4. Exodus 20:17 (above), is the second moral commandment that applies to marriage. The desire (lust or covetousness) being for-

144

bidden isn't sexual desire; sexual desire is a natural part of human life. The forbidden lust is described by Exodus 20:17 as first seeing a woman, like your neighbor's wife, as though she were in the same category as any other <u>thing</u> your neighbor <u>owns</u>. The forbidden sexual lust then desires to take that woman and use her for personal gratification as though she were a just a possession, or as we might say in contemporary language, to use her as a sexual object. Neither a woman nor a man is a possession which can be owned, or a sexual object which can be used as a tool for gratification. What is the difference between sexually gratifying each other and using each other as a tool of gratification?

5. A woman is not a house, or an ox, or a donkey, or even a servant. Both a woman and a man are persons whose rights must be honored; human beings who deserve to be sexually treasured. What might it mean to sexually treasure your marriage partner?

6. Perhaps the quintessential example of sexual lust is the story of David and Bathsheba (II Samuel 12:1–5). David is a king and a powerful man capable of making things happen. From the high roof of his Jerusalem house, he looks out and sees a beautiful woman bathing on the roof of her home. This woman is Bathsheba. David is consumed with the desire to sexually possess Bathsheba. He doesn't care about what she wants or about the impact of his behavior on her life. David has her brought to his bed, has sex with her, and then sends her home. David neither sees nor treats Bathsheba as a person with rights to be honored. He uses her sexually and sends her away. How do you judge David's behavior towards Bathsheba?

3. <u>Treat the one you love as sacred.</u>

When we realize people are sacred to God we learn to treat ourselves and each other as sacred. That is why we neither sexually violate nor betray ourselves or each other.

(1 Corinthians 6:13–20)

<u>For the Pastor / Counselor:</u>

Paul's argument in 1 Corinthians 6:13–20 against using prostitutes is a striking one. He doesn't reference the commandment against adultery which condemns sexual unfaithfulness. It might be expected that a Jew trained in Hebrew law would base a moral argument regarding sexual behavior on the commandments. Instead, Paul bases his argument on the sacred (or holy) nature of a Christian's relationship with God in Christ. Let us deconstruct the points of Paul's argument . . . not necessarily in order. By paraphrasing his argument, it becomes clear that Paul hits the following four points. (Note the word 'sacred' or 'holy' is not in this text, but its meaning runs throughout it. By definition, sacred means belonging to God and set aside for God's purposes.)

1) Now that Christ has bought you, your body is *sacred* to God. This means God is meant for your body, and your body is meant for God. Your body is not meant for sexual immorality but to glorify God.

2) Because we are part of the Body of Christ our bodies are *sacred* members of Christ. It would be unthinkable to make your *sacred* bodies members with a prostitute.

3) Our bodies are *sacred* to God. As Christ was raised from death so our bodies will be raised by God's power. Run from sexual immorality; it is a sin against your own body.

4) We are joined to the Lord; and our spirits are one with his. But if you visit a prostitute, you become "one body" with her; for sex makes two people "one flesh." Your body is a *sacred* temple of God in which God the

Holy Spirit lives. How can you make God's *Holy* Spirit "one flesh" with a prostitute?

Questions to discuss with the couple:

7. Sacred (or holy) means belonging to God and set aside for God's purposes. Your body is sacred (holy) to God and your partner's body is sacred (holy) to God. What are some ways a couple might treat each other that shows they *do* hold each other as physically and sexually sacred?

8. The reason we don't sexually violate ourselves or our partner is we recognize both of us are sacred to God. We don't sexually betray ourselves or our partner for the same reason. What are some ways couples treat each other that might show they *do not* hold each other as physically and sexually sacred?

4. **Realize that married sex is God-blessed.**

All human relationships, including every human sexual relationship, are infected by sin. The Good News is when married couples love each other as does God, with a faithful love (like Christ's love for the church), their sexual relationship has God's blessing. God wants to free married couples from any idea their sex lives are evil, or dirty, or anything but God-blessed.

(Romans 3:10 – 18, Ephesians 5:21 – 33, Hebrews 13:4)

For the Pastor / Counselor:

The third section of this book, "A Study Paper," entitled, "With a Christ-Like Love," discusses the doctrine of sin and its implications for understanding intimate human relationships. Two points from that discussion are relevant here. 1) The best of human relationships are warped by sin, including our most loving sexual relationships – no matter the sexual orientation. 2) For that reason, no one can claim their sexual relationship is superior because it is pure or sin free. However, Hebrews chapter thirteen, verse 4, teaches, even though sin warps all human relationships, faithful married sex is blessed by God. The message of the Hebrews passage is that God will consider our marriages honorable and our sexual relationships morally pure if we are sexually faithful.

Ephesians chapter five, verses 25 to 27 teaches a similar lesson, but obliquely. On first reading, it may seem the passage is going to argue that husbands can sanctify their relationship with their wives by loving them faithfully as Christ loved the church. But that is not the message. The passage focuses on Christ's love, which sanctifies and cleanses the church making it "without stain, wrinkle or blemish." Although the passage compares the love between husbands and wives to the faithful and sacrificial love between Christ and the Church, it is not their faithful love for each other that sanctifies the marriage relationship.

The Ephesians Five text sets up a parallel construction, comparing the faithful sacrificial love of Christ for the church (the mystery about which the author speaks in this passage, Ephesians 5:32); and the faithful, Christ-like love which Christian husbands and wives are to have for each other. The text tells husbands to love their wives as their own bodies, just like Christ loves, feeds, and cares for his body the church (Ephesians 5:28-29). Marital love is further tied to the love of Christ for the church by the concluding statement of verse 30, "Because we (i.e. Christian husbands and wives) are members of his body."

As members of Christ's body, the church which consists of Christian individuals, we are cleansed of sin and made without stain, wrinkle or blemish. Through use of parallel construction, the text teaches a new idea: a Christian couple who loves each other with a faithful, Christ like love is also cleansed of sin because they are part of Christ's body. It is not simply by sharing a faithful, Christ like love that a Christian couple is cleansed or sanctified. It is that the married couple are members together of Christ's body, and as such are declared by Christ to be without stain, wrinkle or blemish – both as individuals and as a married couple.

It should be clear that what sanctifies a marriage, and claims God's blessing, is not that it joins the lives of a man and a woman. A marriage is not blessed by God because it is a heterosexual pairing. God's blessing on human sexual relationships is pred-icated on sexual faithfulness. The message of the Ephesians text is that marriage between two Christians who are mem-bers of Christ's body, and who love each other with Christ-like faithfulness, is a sanctified relationship. The faithful sexual re-lationship of two Christian people, because they are members of Christ's body, is God-blessed.

Questions to discuss with the couple:

9. Is there ever any reason for a Christian couple to think their sexual relationship is evil, or dirty, or anything but God-blessed? Why or why not?

10. The faithful sexual relationship of Christian couple is blessed by God. Does sexual unfaithfulness revoke God's blessing on a Christian couple's sexual relationship? Why or why not?

11. If there is sexual unfaithfulness in a marriage, what can allow a fresh beginning, forgiveness, healing, and cleansing? Have you (for any reason) had to go through an experience of betrayal and reconciliation while dating? How did you handle the experience?

12. How does it feel to imagine your Christian Marriage will only last a lifetime if neither of you makes big mistakes? How does it feel to imagine you will make many marriage mistakes which will re-

quire you as a couple to stop and renegotiate your marriage to meet changing feelings, needs and desires? Do you envision your marriage as the successful run of a life-long marathon; or as the successful run of many sprints, with numerous stops and numerous new beginnings? Which vision is more realistic? Which would be easier?

13. Being pushed to anger is not a threat to emotional well being; it is a normal part of the course of love. But can forgiveness ever be appropriate when there has been a realistic threat to your physical health or emotional well being? Why or why not?

5. Be unashamed of your loving feelings and affection.

When the love between two people is vibrant and healthy they neither desire to hide their love from friends nor want to withdraw themselves from society – either out of shame or guilt or out of a desire for secrecy. They are proud and unashamed to express their feelings of love.

(Song of Solomon 8:1)

For the Pastor / Counselor:

The Song of Solomon is a good example of Wisdom literature that gives guidance to marriages. It doesn't give commands. It doesn't recommend behavior because it is wise or because it will create marital happiness. Instead, the Song of Solomon gives narrative examples of loving statements which two people in love might share with each other. Verses 1 and 2 of the eighth chapter of the Song of Solomon, illustrate two of the most important indicators of strong and healthy romantic love. Verse 1 says, "Oh that you were like a brother to me, who nursed at my mother's breasts! If I found you outside, I would kiss you, and none would despise me." The verse expresses the healthy, unashamed desire of romantic love to openly show its affectionate feelings when around family and friends. It expresses the appropriate desire for its affection to be accepted and respected.

Questions to discuss with the couple:

14. A healthy romantic love is proud to be openly affectionate in front of loved ones. Have you ever been tempted to sneak behind the backs of, or hide your romantic relationship from family and friends? Is there a set of relatives or friends around whom you don't feel free to express your affection? Why do you think this might be?

15. Respond to this statement. If you feel guilty before your family about being with the one you love, or feel the need to keep your romantic relationship secret, think carefully before deciding to marry him or her.

LESSON FOUR

Class Opening

> (Leader) Gracious God, (pray in unison) **teach us to love each other as a couple with a Christ-like love. Teach us to know each other as Christ knows us. Teach us to take joy in each other as Christ takes joy in us.**
>
> **When love gets hard, let us be patient with each other as you are patient. Let us strive to be understanding as you understand. Let us be faithful to each other as you are faithful.**
>
> **Grant that through our shared successes and failures, through our shared happiness and sorrow, we might find lasting joy in the lessons of love which you teach us. We pray in the name of Jesus Christ, who shows us your love, calls us to love, and empowers us with your love. Amen**

1) Ask the icebreaker question. (See the Guide for Clergy introduction.)

2) Begin with the discussion questions you've chosen for this session.

The Discipline of Family Love: 6 – 9

6. <u>Involve the one you love in your family.</u>

Married love is not just a private matter between two people. At its heart, it involves expanding family ties and extending the reach of a family's love to include new people. Couples need to share their lives and their love with members of their extended families.

(Song of Solomon 8:2)

For the Pastor / Counselor: The second indicator of a strong and vital romantic love, as described by The Song of Solomon, is located in chapter 8, verse 2: "I would lead you and bring you into the house of my mother — she who used to teach me." This verse illustrates another important principle. Marriage is not only about starting a new family. Husbands and wives need not only to separate themselves from their parents (Ephesians 5:31). Marriage is about extending one's family of origin. Newly married husbands and wives need to find a way to embrace each other's family (i.e. to take each other home to their parents.) And the parent's role is similar. Parents need to find a way to embrace their children's new married family.

Questions to discuss with the couple:

1. What questions do you have from the Couple's Pamphlet or from the Couple's Letter(s)? Ask the couple or couples, "Is there homework from our last session? Are there questions that have come to your mind since we last met or talked?" Share homework.

2. Do your parents extend to you the right to marry the person you love and to bring that person into their extended family? How do they express their welcome, or rejection?

3. Would you freely welcome into your family the person your child chooses to marry? What might cause you to withhold your blessing or welcome? If either of your in-laws do not welcome your marriage, be patient and forgiving. How would you feel about politely avoiding them while hoping their attitude will change? Is there another approach to unwelcoming in-laws which you might take?

4. How do you feel about including your parents and in-laws in the extended family formed by your marriage? How would you feel should your parents resist being included in your family, or circumstances (such as distance) make this impossible?

7. <u>**Find ways to give creative expression to your love.**</u>

All families need to find ways to express their love. This can involve parenting children and nurturing social causes. It certainly will involve giving support to and receiving support from other families in the Christian faith community.

(Psalms 128:3; I Corinthians 12:24-26; Romans 16:10-11; I Peter 4:9)

<u>For the Pastor / Counselor:</u>

Psalm 128:3 reads, "Your wife will be like a fruitful vine within your house; your children will be like olive shoots around your table." The primary meaning of this verse is that God's blessing will show itself through a fertile wife and many children. This verse expresses the essential creative and fertile nature of a married couple's love. For that reason, it is important to extend the meaning of this verse to couples without children and to those whose children are grown. This passage enables us to say their love will also seek *to give birth*, to *parent, and to nurture*. If a couple does not have children, does not adopt children, or their children have left home, or they marry past the age when they are interested in or able to give birth to children, they will seek other ways to be creative and give of themselves. They may volunteer individually or as a couple in community activities. They may give their time and energy to a social cause they believe in. They may express their creative, nurturing energy through church ministry. All of these are valid ways in which a couple may express the fertile energy of their love.

Christian married couples will also give nurture or support to, and receive support from, the other couples in their community. This includes couples in their faith community first and then includes couples in their wider community (Galatians

6:10). One of the primary functions of a Christian wedding is to give social recognition and welcome to the new couple by other community couples. First Corinthians 12:24-26, which describes the body of Christ, is commonly interpreted to apply to individual Christians. Each individual Christian is an indispensable part of the Christianity community. However, since the term "body" in the text refers to the Christian community, there's no reason the passage shouldn't equally embrace married couples and families. Christian married couples and families are also indispensable parts of the Christian Community.

The I Corinthians text says, "God has so composed the body, giving greater honor to the part that lacked it, that there may be no division in the body, but that the members may have the same care for one another. If one member suffers, all suffer together; if one member is honored, all rejoice together." If the word "member" in the text were interpreted to mean both individuals and families, the sense would be unchanged. Christian hospitality is important (I Peter 4:9), and cannot be limited only to individuals. It's worth noting in this context that Paul's final greetings in the book of Romans includes his well-wishes to both individuals and households (Romans 16:10-11). Like Paul, we need to recognize each other's households and put into action our "care for one another" as families.

<u>Questions to discuss with the couple</u>:

5. Married love is essentially nurturing and creative. How do you feel about making it a first priority in your life to nurture your partner? Can you imagine giving yourself to nurture your partner, not only without losing yourself, but actually becoming more yourself?

6. What interests do you both support as a couple that energize you both?

7. What are ways you as a couple would enjoy giving yourselves to others, to the church, to your community?

155

8. <u>**Learn how to love someone who is different.**</u>

It is natural to be drawn to a life partner who has a supplementary and even opposite personality characteristics. Christian Marriage challenges life partners to embrace each other with the kind of love that values and treasures a person for the ways in which they are different.

See Isaiah 55:8-9, which says, "My thoughts are not your thoughts, neither are your ways my ways, declares the Lord."

For the Pastor / Counselor:

The attraction of love for someone who is excitingly different from ourselves is an often observed human experience and it is a well-supported biblical insight. I'll not address the literature of psychology, but I'll note the popular aphorism, "Opposites attract." However, this principle is clearly illustrated by God's love for humans. Isaiah 55:8-9 says that God's ways are different from human ways . . . as different as earth is from sky. The principle is also illustrated in the primary scriptural descriptions of marriage. In both Genesis and Ephesians, marriage is described as a relationship between different sexes, between a man and a woman. As noted in "The Study Paper," a Christian Marriage need not be between a man and woman. But married love does need to be an essential attraction between people who are different.

In fact, being of different sexes may not be enough of a difference to make a marriage work. A relationship between a man and woman whose personalities are too similar may feel almost incestuous. And a love relationship between two people of the same-sex needs to pay attention to the same principle. The one you love enough to marry needs to have a personality style which is different from your own, with characteristics both supplementary and opposite to yours. One important goal of Christian Marriage is to enable both partners to learn to love each other for the ways *they are different*.

Questions to discuss with the couple:

8. What likes, preferences and instincts do you see in yourself you do not see in your partner? What strengths do you see in your partner you do not see in yourself?

9. Give examples of situations in which the two of you would have made different decisions or responded very differently.

10. Can you imagine learning to enjoy each other's differences?

11. Are your worship preferences similar and compatible? In what ways?

12. Have you discussed how you would want to handle the religious training of your children? How is the vision you have for the religious training of children, should you have them, similar or not similar?

9. Expect love to provoke you to grow and change.

Persons different enough to fascinate us and win our love may provoke and even infuriate us. A life partner can do more than complete us with strengths we need – but do not have. They will also provoke us to deal with issues we need to face – but want to avoid.

(Ephesians 4:26)

For the Pastor / Counselor:

A perfectly loving world would not be smooth going or trouble free. Love's character is to reach out to embrace one who is different. Those differences, which may initially charm and attract us, can become the source of irritation, misunderstanding, and hard feelings. Behind those charming differences may be very different assumptions about what's important in life, or different expectations for how conflict is to be expressed and resolved. Quite often the person with whom you fell in love will have a very different style of communicating their feelings and expressing what is important to them.

Because understanding is so important, and misunderstanding between people is so easy, Scripture tells couples to give highest priority to working through problems that cause anger and to do it before going to bed. The anger that deals with its cause right away avoids sin (Ephesians 4:26). So, don't let misunderstanding fester. Make a strong effort to break down communication barriers as they arise.

Scripture indicates there is a distinct difference between positive anger that leads to solving problems and destructive anger that damages everything it touches. Destructive anger, sometimes called wrath, rage, malice, or bitterness, is to be avoided (Ephesians 4:31; Colossians 3:8). But when Jesus was criticized for healing a man on the Sabbath, Mark's Gospel compares his anger to grief (Mark 3:1 - 6). And the anger of Jesus at the religious vendors in the temple courts is called zeal (John 2:14-17). Zeal can also be described as fervent devotion. It is important to note both grief and devotion can be understood as expressions of love. It is important for the understanding of positive anger to see it as an expression of love. We could say positive anger is the energy love gives us to confront interpersonal problems, hurt feelings, and betrayals. When our feelings are hurt, we need this energy to ask why we feel hurt and to confront and deal with the bruised relationship.

Questions to discuss with the couple:

13. Why might it be better to judge the strength of your romantic relationship on the quality of your arguments rather than on the passion of your intimacy?

14. Is it your goal to avoid argument, or to develop together the skill of loving and helpful argument?

15. Discuss the following outline of a strategy for loving argument.

    - If you can feel your anger rising, and realize you are about to initiate an argument in your relationship, decide to use the energy your anger gives you to determine exactly what you feel and what actions triggered those negative feelings.

    - Put in words to yourself how you feel hurt, or violated, or misunderstood. This will not be easy because bruised feelings are vulnerable feelings and hard to express.

    - Use your anger energy to risk expressing your hurt or violated or misunderstood feelings without placing blame.

    - Then ask for your partner's understanding and empathy.

16. Is it better to resolve an argument with an apology or with understanding? Discuss the following observation. When feelings are wounded, an apology is often not enough. Nothing heals wounded feelings like knowing the one who has hurt you has also put in the effort to understand your hurt – from your point of view.

LESSON FIVE

Class Opening

> (Leader) Gracious God, (pray in unison) **teach us to love each other as a couple with a Christ-like love. Teach us to know each other as Christ knows us. Teach us to take joy in each other as Christ takes joy in us.**
>
> **When love gets hard, let us be patient with each other as you are patient. Let us strive to be understanding as you understand. Let us be faithful to each other as you are faithful.**
>
> **Grant that through our shared successes and failures, through our shared happiness and sorrow, we might find lasting joy in the lessons of love which you teach us. We pray in the name of Jesus Christ, who shows us your love, calls us to love, and empowers us with your love. Amen**

1) Ask the icebreaker question. (See the Guide for Clergy introduction.)

2) Begin with the discussion questions you've chosen for this session.

The Discipline of Family Love: 10

10. <u>Strive to build a lasting love relationship.</u>

Commit yourself to building a lasting love relationship that treasures its first joy, seeks understanding and reconciliation when there is conflict, admits when its actions cause hurt, takes pleasure in mutual self-revelation, and does all it can to foster an enduring bond of honesty and trust.

<u>For the Pastor / Counselor</u>:

The narrative of Biblical History tells the developing story of love between God and God's people as the divine / human love relationship goes through the following six phases or movements. Phases 1 – 5 are discussed here in Lesson Five. Phase 6 is discussed in Lesson Six. God's love for humanity, as revealed in Scripture, shows us the pattern or phases involved in building a strong and lasting love.

The following phases or steps describe the process of working through relationship problems as small as a misunderstanding, or as large as severely hurt feelings. They describe how a relationship can move from conflict to reconciliation and healing. By regularly working through these steps a couple can steadily move towards building a strong and lasting love relationship.

(1) Remember and focus on your early love when harmony and joy prevailed. Imagine recapturing that time.

<u>For the Pastor / Counselor</u>:

The story of God's love relationship with humanity begins in a garden paradise with a relationship of perfect harmony. When there is discord in the divine / human relationship, the Eden story calls us to remember a time when harmony and joy prevailed. It also encourages us to look forward to a time when harmony and joy will be restored.

<u>Questions to discuss with the couple</u>:

1. What questions do you have from the Couple's Pamphlet or from the Couple's Letter(s)? Ask the couple or couples, "Is there homework from our last session? Are there questions that have come to your mind since we last met or talked?" Share homework.

2. When you have had an argument, or serious unhappiness, have you tried recalling and treasuring the joy you had at the beginning of your relationship? Would looking back on good times help you get through hard or painful times?

3. What would it take for you as a couple to remember and recapture your first joy?

4. What if you as a couple are not able to go back to your original joy? This need not be a loss. Discuss the following statement. You can challenge yourselves to go *forward to a new joy* that can account for and build on the totality of your experiences.

(2)   Seek reconciliation.

For the Pastor / Counselor:

Biblical History can also be seen as the working out of God's attempt and humanity's struggle to build bridges of understanding and reconciliation in the sin-broken God-human relationship. The Old Testament tells the story of the failed human attempt to heal that relationship through right behavior and right worship. Neither effort worked. The human struggle to obey God through right behavior, is like a marriage partner promising to try to always be good and to never mess up. The human struggle to please God through right worship is like a marriage partner flattering, praising, and giving gifts. These strategies are not very effective long-term.

Questions to discuss with the couple:

5. When, if ever, might your promises to "mend your ways" help your love relationship grow?

6. When, if ever, might your willingness to give your partner sincere flattery, unexpected praise, and surprise gifts, help your love relationship grow?

7. Do such behaviors help more when you are trying to heal bruised feelings or when done out of a generous heart when things are going well in your marriage relationship?

(3)   Reconciliation begins with building understanding.

For the Pastor / Counselor:

The cross of Jesus Christ is an example of effective reconciliation. Without talking about the cross as a saving event, we can look at how it is a pattern for healing a broken love relationship. To the extent we can see the cross as a statement that reveals God's love for us, we can see on the cross the vivid picture of God showing humanity how our sin causes God pain and suffering (See BoC 9.09 & 9.15). When a human relationship has been damaged, one of the involved persons has to communicate their pain. One partner has to say to the other, "Let me tell you how badly I am hurt." The relationship is healed when the other person understands the magnitude of the hurt they caused and undergoes a change of heart that allows them to see their relationship differently.

Questions to discuss with the couple:

8. When your feelings are hurt how do you feel when your partner apologizes and says, "I'm sorry?"

9. Discuss the following observation. Healing empathy cannot take place unless the person who is hurt expresses, clearly, calmly, and without placing blame, the pain they feel.

10. When your feelings are hurt, how would you feel if your partner listens empathetically, communicates they understand the depth of your hurt, and lets you know they are willing to be changed by their understanding?

(4)   Offer confession and extend empathy.

<u>For the Pastor / Counselor:</u>

Love admits when its actions cause hurt. This is the New Testament concept of confession. In the first chapter of the first epistle of John, the topic is fellowship – the fellowship of Christians with each other and the fellowship of Christians with God (I John 1:3). John explains that God is light and our fellowship with God and each other requires us to walk in light *and truth* (I John 1:5-7). That is why, says John, our fellowship with God and each other breaks down when we indulge in the religious pretense that we are perfect people, without sin. This kind of religious pretense is false and represents neither honesty nor truth (I John 1:8). An honest and truthful relationship with God and with fellow Christians is maintained by what John calls confession.

Scriptural confession isn't like a legal allocution of wrongdoing before a judge. It isn't a simple admission of wrongdoing. Scriptural confession requires empathy. It means seeing one's actions, from the viewpoint of the one you are confessing to, and telling that person what you see in yourself. We maintain our fellowship with God by looking at our actions from God's perspective and telling God in prayer what we see. We maintain our social fellowship when there is conflict between ourselves and another Christian, by looking at our actions from that person's point of view, and, telling them what we see.

<u>Questions to discuss with the couple</u>:

11. We first learn to argue from our parents, then later from our friends and loved ones. Can you give an example of an important argument which you witnessed or were involved in that was ended by understanding and empathy?

12. Can you give an example of an important argument in which your complaint was met by confession?

13. What makes it hard for you to think about what you have said or done from your partner's viewpoint, see how you have caused hurt, and then tell your partner what you've discovered about yourself? (Confession)

14. When you have hurt the one you love, and catch yourself doing it, or your loved one confronts you with their hurt, what is your first response? What might your best response be?

(5)   Embrace the joy of self-revelation.

For the Pastor / Counselor:

Love takes pleasure in mutual self-revelation. The Old and New Testaments, taken together, is not only a story of the reconciliation of a broken relationship between God and humanity, it is the story of God's continued efforts at self-disclosure. As Christians, when we learn to see God as love, we are able to understand God's ongoing efforts at self-revelation as an extension of God's love (BoC 9.15; 9.41).

If we take Genesis as a record of God's first attempts to be known to humanity, then God's initial self-disclosure was as Creator. To Abraham, God is the one who calls him to follow, and promises to bless his family. To Jacob, God is the one with whom he wrestles all night. To Joseph, God is the one who rescues him from slavery and prison, and uses him to bless both the nation of Egypt and his eleven brothers. To Moses, God is YHWH, who is "I am who I am" (Exodus 3:14); and the one who leads the nation of Israel on the road to Exodus. To the people of Israel wandering in the wilderness, God is a guide in the form of a cloud by day and a pillar of fire by night. God gives a unique self-revelation to Israel through Moses in the form of Moral law, Civil law, and Judicial law. During and after the reign of King David, God was known as King of Creation. The Jewish prophets of the later kingdom era developed the idea God's reign included God's desire for mercy and justice.

In the New Testament, God takes an entirely new step towards self-revelation, an ultimate and complete self-revelation in the man Jesus (BoC 9.27), in whom God was incarnate, completely present and active. The self-disclosure of God in Jesus is relevant in this context. In his Gospel, John tells his readers when we look at Jesus, we see God's Word who became flesh (i.e. human), to show us the glory of God the Father (John 1:14). The author of II Corinthians makes a similar point. When we look at Christ we see God. And when the light of God shines in our hearts, we are able to experience the knowledge of God's glory shining from the person of Christ (II Corinthians 4:4-6).

<u>Questions to discuss with the couple</u>:

15. Is the "getting to know you" stage of your marriage relationship over or is it something that still keeps giving you joy? What has triggered a recent "getting to know you" moment?

16. Identify what you struggle with when you try to disclose yourself (your feelings, thoughts, and convictions) to your partner?

17. What is the most effective thing you have learned to do to help your partner reveal themselves (their feelings, thoughts, and convictions) to you?

18. Discuss the following observation. Love takes pleasure in revealing itself and rejoices in the revealing of its partner.

LESSON SIX

Class Opening

> (Leader) Gracious God, (pray in unison) **teach us to love each other as a couple with a Christ-like love. Teach us to know each other as Christ knows us. Teach us to take joy in each other as Christ takes joy in us.**
>
> **When love gets hard, let us be patient with each other as you are patient. Let us strive to be understanding as you understand. Let us be faithful to each other as you are faithful.**
>
> **Grant that through our shared successes and failures, through our shared happiness and sorrow, we might find lasting joy in the lessons of love which you teach us. We pray in the name of Jesus Christ, who shows us your love, calls us to love, and empowers us with your love. Amen**

1) Ask the icebreaker question. (See the Guide for Clergy introduction.)

2) Begin with the discussion questions you've chosen for this session.

The Discipline of Family Love: **10 (cont.)**

10 (cont.) Strive to Build a Lasting Love Relationship

(6) Create an enduring bond of trust and honesty.

> For the Pastor / Counselor:
>
> The love relationship between God and God's people is described many ways within Scripture. However, two particular and important aspects of the human relationship with God

that apply directly to married couples are trust and honesty. In much of Protestant theology and popular preaching since the Reformation, the human relationship with God is described in terms of faith, faithfulness, and ***trust***. A strong love relationship with God, and a strong marriage relationship, both require a foundation of trust.

Protestant churches have historically stood for *salvation by faith* (or trust in God). And the historic English wedding vow follows suit by having the participants promise *faith* or *fidelity* to each other. The archaic wording is, "I plight thee *my troth*," which means, "I pledge to you my faith (or faithfulness)." "I give you my faith doesn't mean, "I have confidence in you." It means, "I pledge my *personal fidelity* to you;" or "I promise *to be true* to you." The faith we place in God that underlies our love relationship with God is epitomized by the moment in the wedding service when the couple promises to give themselves to each other. The faith that supports both the love relationship with God, and the love relationship that constitutes marriage, is the faith that says "I do" to the promise of personal fidelity.

When faith and trust are broken, both parties in a marriage relationship will want to work towards reconciliation, using skills we discussed previously, through confession, understanding, and empathy. This brings up the second important aspect of a strong love relationship: honesty. Both love for God and marriage love require honesty. Another New Testament word that frequently occurs in association with the human relationship with God relates to honesty: "homologeo." It carries two meanings in New Testament Greek: to honestly agree or confess (as in confess your sins); and to honestly profess (as in proclaim your faith). In practical terms, both meanings of this word describe the role of honesty in relationships: the honesty to face and discuss the wrongs you've done and the honesty to share your deepest feelings, convictions and values.

We have already discussed confession, or confession of sin, as a vehicle for bringing honest understanding together with empathy. Perhaps the most familiar reference to this kind of confession is in the first epistle of John, chapter 1, verse 9 – a verse we have also previously discussed. To recap, the context of the passage is fellowship between Christians and God, and between Christians. The act that restores fellowship when a sin has interrupted the intimacy of a relationship, is honesty. Confession is the kind of honesty that continually tries to build bridges of understanding. Honest confession heals relationships by bringing the power of empathy to bear on hurt feelings.

The other meaning of "homologeo" is to profess what you believe. Romans 10:9-10 describes the human relationship with God as consisting of confessing and believing. This kind of confessing involves the honest sharing of your most important values and beliefs. Believing in the sense described here is the trust that makes a relationship real and lasting.

> **If you confess with your mouth that Jesus is Lord and believe in your heart that God raised him from the dead, you will be saved. For with the heart one believes and is justified, and with the mouth one confesses and is saved. (Romans 10:9-10)**

A strong love relationship with God, and a strong marriage relationship both require the kind of honesty that speaks openly about hurts that arise, seeks understanding, and strives for empathy. Both loves encompass a love that shares its most important values and convictions. Both love relationships require an ongoing trust. And, when trust is broken, both parties seek reconciliation through confession, understanding, and empathy.

<u>Questions to discuss with the couple</u>:

<u>Questions about trust</u>

1. What questions do you have from the Couple's Pamphlet or from the Couple's Letter(s)? Ask the couple or couples, "Is there homework from our last session? Are there questions that have come to your mind since we last met or talked?" Share homework.

2. What moves you to trust your partner? What gets in the way of trust?

3. Since you've known each other, what has happened to put stress on your trust in each other? How did you restore the trust between yourselves?

<u>Questions about confession</u>

4. Do you believe lashing out in anger a) clears the air, or b) makes it harder for your partner to listen to you? Explain your answer.

5. When you explain your hurt feelings, you believe you should a) explain clearly why your hurt is your partner's fault so they cannot escape their responsibility, or b) risk honestly telling your partner how you feel – without placing blame?

6. Is it better to a) use all the energy and bravery which anger can give you to nail your partner to the wall, or b) use the energy of your anger to risk telling the person who has hurt you how wounded you feel?

7. The best approach is to a) say you're sorry as fast as you can to get the argument out of the way, or b) after you have listened with understanding and empathy, and re-established trust, then say you are sorry.

Questions about profession

8. "Profession" means a) sharing Christ's Good News with your partner, or b) regularly sharing your deepest values and most important convictions with your partner?

9. A marriage relationship survives long term a) because the couple has learned to enjoy sharing "small talk," or b) because they've learned to keep on sharing and discussing their personal beliefs, or c) both?

10. Daily life is easier a) when you can interject profound issues to discuss, or b) when you can honestly share your thoughts and feelings in reaction to the events of the day?

Concluding QUESTIONS and ANSWERS about Christian Marriage

Q. How does a couple enter into Christian Marriage?

A. Christian Marriage begins when two people promise before God to love each other exclusively for as long as they live and express their commitment through sexual union. Christian Marriage is consecrated when the church celebrates the joining of these two lives through a Christian wedding which publicly recognizes their place as a married couple within the Christian faith community.

For the Pastor / Counselor:

Scripture has much to say about marriage but little to say about weddings. The Presbyterian Directory of Worship describes Christian Marriage with the words, "Marriage involves a unique commitment between two people, traditionally a man and a woman, to love and support each other for the rest of their lives (W-4.9001)." It describes civil marriage, with the words, "In civil law, marriage is a contract that recognizes the rights and obligations of the couple in society" (W-4.9002).

The third section of this book, *Preparing for Christian Marriage*, "The Study Paper," attempts to clarify the distinction between the contract of civil marriage, as codified in state law, and the spiritual values of Christian Marriage as described in Scripture and the Presbyterian Creeds.

What does Scripture say about how marriage is entered into? Let's examine those few passages that give us a clue. Genesis 2:24 doesn't describe the marriage of Adam and Eve as an event but describes a fundamental rationale for marriage. In the next chapter, in Genesis 3:8, Adam and Eve are described as married, as husband and wife. Their *wedding* by implication involved them uniting with or "holding fast to" each other with God as their witness. No one else was present to witness their marriage nor was anyone else needed. They entered into marriage by cleaving or joining their lives together in the sight of God.

Did their sexual relationship begin at this point? Scripture doesn't pinpoint when Adam and Eve began sexual relations. In Genesis 4:1, Scripture indicates, as a result of their sexual relationship, Adam and Eve gave birth to their first child. However, as Reformed Christians, we do not believe human sexual relationships are an artifact of the fall of Adam and Eve or of human sin. We consequently have no reason to think human sexual relationships began only after humanity left Eden. We do not hold sex is, in itself, a sinful activity, or human birth is a result of sinful activity, or sex passes on sin from parents to children.

Reformed Christians believe faithful human sexual relationships are God-blessed. The Second Helvetic Confession beautifully describes married sexual relations as instituted and blessed by God.

For marriage (which is the medicine of incontingency, and contingency itself) was instituted by the Lord God himself, who blessed it most bountifully, and willed man and woman to cleave one to the other inseparably, and to live together in complete love and concord (BoC 5.246; see also BoC 6.131).

Neither Scripture nor the Reformed Creeds directly state sexual relations are a constituent part of Marriage. In the Study Paper, we noted Christian Marriages need not be procreative. Still, marriage and sex are linked in Scripture. Clearly, marriage is constituted when "two people promise before God to love each other exclusively for as long as they live." Also clearly, the couple's promise to join their lives *can be* expressed by sexual congress.

In the book of Ruth, the marriage of Ruth and Boaz is described as a two part process. First Boaz acquires Ruth as his wife (Ruth 4:10); then the two have sexual relations (Ruth 4:13). In the book of Esther, the marriage between Esther and the King Ahasuerus is given expression in a more public way, by a huge feast (Esther 2:18). The parables of Jesus describe marriage in a similar way. Jesus refers to marriage primarily in terms of a festive marriage feast or banquet. It would be a strange and strained interpretation of Scripture to suggest Christian couples need to give expression to their marriage by holding a marriage feast. Of course, they may if they choose to hold a marriage feast or banquet; and many do. But the question is whether it would be equally strange or strained to suggest sexual relations are a natural expression of marriage? No. There is evidence within Scripture the connection between marriage and sex is a reasonable one.

In chapter twenty two of Deuteronomy, several scenarios are described in which a man's sexual relations with a woman would be improper. For each scenario, a punishment or consequence is stated. In verses 28–29, the scenario is this. An unmarried man has sex with unmarried woman while the two are by themselves out of town or in the field. The consequence described is real, but not frightening. The man has to pay the girl's father 50 silver shekels which is half the fine for ruining the reputation of a virgin (Deuteronomy 22:19). He has to take the woman as his wife and may not divorce her. It is commonly suggested this passage describes the consequences of rape. Its meaning would then be that rape constitutes marriage and the marriage formed by rape must last for the life of the woman. This is a possible interpretation.

However, all the other penalties described in this chapter of Deuteronomy are much more severe. The scale of penalties range upwards from a fine of 100 silver shekels and punishment by the girl's father to death by stoning. It might be that in Deuteronomy 22:28-29, rape is considered a lesser crime, deserving a much lesser penalty. But there may be something else going on in this passage. It would not be a stretch to suppose Hebrew rapists were predatory brutes. Rape is a brutish and predatory crime often not discovered or reported because the rapist secretly terrorizes and threatens his victim to keep silent. This passage from Deuteronomy chapter 22 proceeds with the assumption that the sexual encounter which takes place out in the countryside becomes known. It may be the rapists in question are not particularly bright or careful, and plan their attacks where they can be observed. Or it might be the sex is consensual and is self-reported by the couple.

The possibility of consensual sex is not mentioned in the Deuteronomy passage because human sex is described throughout Old Testament Scripture as something exclusively in the man's power and the man's responsibility. But the book of Ruth provides a clear example of a sexual overture initiated by a young woman that then led to marriage. Clearly not all Hebrew women were sexually passive. Because of the example of Ruth, we know being a Hebrew woman of good character did not always necessitate sexual passivity. Add to this a general knowledge of human nature and it becomes reasonable to suggest this passage can apply to consensual sex, desired by both the young man and the young woman. In that case, the text would mean if two young people want each other, and when they are together out in the countryside can't wait to have sex, provision is made for them. When they return to town, they approach the girl's father and explain their situation. They give her father 50 shekels and are considered a married couple.

Whether this text describes rape, or the impetuous sexual tryst of a hot-blooded young couple, the result is the same. The couple is to be married. The implication seems to be that a commitment to be married might better come before beginning sexual relations. But, if the sexual relationship begins first, the couple then becomes acceptable in the sight of God and their community by taking the necessary steps to marry each other. The second and clear implication of the text is that a marriage may begin with the man making the proper negotiations with the girl's father before sexual relations commence. However, if sexual relations occur first, the couple's sexual congress is taken to be an expression of marriage and the couple can satisfy propriety, God, and society by doing what is necessary to be wed and make their marriage public.

Not every two people who have sexual intercourse intend to begin a lifelong marriage commitment. They may intend a onetime experience or a casual relationship with an "on again off again" sexual component. How does the Deuteronomy passage apply to these folk? Do Christians believe every couple who has sex should get married, as this text seems to imply? Or do Christians believe every couple who has sex is already married in God's sight even though they may be unaware of it? Neither is true. Although we may take guidance from Deuteronomy chapter 22, it is an example of Hebrew Judicial Law which we do not believe is intended to govern our lives today. That is, this text is not Moral Law but it does describe an important aspect of human sexual experience.

Here we need to go beyond what the Bible directly says about sexual intercourse. We have to appeal to subjective human experience to fill in our understanding of the relationship between sex and marriage. What we can say is sex can be a profoundly uniting and powerfully binding experience between two people. It can also be trivialized to being no more than mutual masturbation in which two people physically pleasure themselves through the participation of their sexual partner.

Christians have tended to frown on trivialized sex between people fundamentally because it causes them to avoid appreciating themselves and their partner as holy and sacred beings. It has also been suggested trivialized sex is the lust forbidden by the Ten Commandments; that lust is the desire to use your partner as an object for your own pleasure and to be used as an object for your partner's pleasure. It has also been argued that trivialized sex leads to breaking the commandment against adultery. The argument is that any casual sexual partners we have prior to our married sexual partner to whom we pledge to be faithful, are infidelities and sexual betrayals of that marriage partner. The argument is that God calls us to be faithful to our marriage partner before we marry them as well as after we marry them.

Here we run into the problem that sex can be trivialized into being a shared physical pleasuring of ourselves or elevated into the ecstatic physical, emotional, and spiritual union of two people. The problem is not everyone can separate their deepest selves, their emotions, and their very soul from the action of their bodies. A person may plan to experience a mere physical pleasure during sex and end up feeling deeply emotionally connected or even personally merged. Then, when the relationship ends or fades, perhaps as agreed upon, the person who has experienced deep connection now feels desolate, abandoned, violated or betrayed.

I suggest the answer is that sex only signifies marriage when shared between two people who have pledged before God to give themselves to each other for a lifetime. However, I suggest sex outside of marriage is a minefield of confusion. Yes, sex can be trivialized into being no more than a shared physical pleasure. But I suggest it can also create intense unity between two people – even if that was not what they wanted or expected. Does that mean the two people are married or should be married? No. But the dissolving of that unity may feel as violating as though a divorce were happening. The repeated painful dissolution of sexual relationships which were intended to be casual, but ended up being intimate relationships that were ruptured when they ended, can leave serious emotional scars.

Questions to discuss with the couple:

11. What advantage, if any, is there for a couple who makes a life-long commitment to be marriage partners before beginning a sexual relationship?

12. What is the distinction between a Christian Marriage and a Christian Wedding?

13. Discuss the following statement. (It is another way of answering the question above, "How does a couple enter into Christian Marriage?") A Christian Marriage may begin with a Christian Wedding for which the couple makes the proper arrangements with

both families and the church. However, if sexual relations begin first, the couple's sexual congress is taken to be an expression of their marriage in the sight of God. The couple can then satisfy moral "propriety" and society's expectations by making arrangements for a Christian Wedding, through which they make their marriage public, and receive the welcome and blessing of the Christian Faith community.

For the Pastor / Counselor:

The remaining questions and answers are a summary of this book's main points about Christian Marriage. A good way to conclude the class would be to read these final questions and answers out loud together.

Q.   What is the essence of Christian Marriage?

A.   The essential and defining characteristic of Christian Marriage is a commitment between two people to love each other faithfully for a lifetime.

Q.   What is the difference between Christian Marriage and civil marriage?

A.   Christian Marriage is the spiritual union of two people which is recognized by God and validated by the Christian Church. Civil marriage is a legal partnership between two people, which meets the requirements for marriage according to the laws of the state in which the couple resides.

Q.   Who may receive Christian Marriage?

A.   The many blessings of Christian Marriage belong to any couple who shows they want those blessings by willingly accepting all the Disciplines of Family Love.

Q.   What is the purpose of Christian Marriage?

A.   The blessings of Christian Marriage are an essential part of God's plan for human life. At its best, Christian Marriage:

- ☐ Embodies the characteristics of God's love,

- ☐ Is a means through which God transforms a couple into Christ-likeness, and

- ☐ Offers the promise of human fulfillment to a couple and their community.

(Genesis 1:26-28, Exodus 34:6, 1 John 4:16, 2 Corinthians 3:18)

Section 3

An Introduction
to the Study Paper, Entitled
With a Christ-Like Love
Offering

An Invitation for My Fellow Protestants

An Invitation for My Fellow Protestants

All of us as Protestants share a Reformation heritage. I know it is simplistic to divide us into our three historical branches: Reformed, Lutheran, and Anabaptist (or Radical – meaning those churches who sought to reclaim Christianity's *roots*). But as a Presbyterian pastor, I would like to invite my fellow Protestants to look into the Reformed (or Presbyterian) theological tradition. It has a significant contribution to make to our current discussion of Marriage Equality.

There's an important historical reason for this. To explain why, I'm going to take the liberty of describing Protestant history in very broad strokes. I don't mean to slight any individual Protestant group or tradition; I've personally experienced several sides of Protestantism. I grew up as a child in an Assemblies of God church; moved as a teen to a Baptist church; later as an adult joined the Presbyterian church, where I became an ordained minister; and later still I completed doctoral work in one of America's foundational Methodist Universities. I've observed we Protestants are deeply individually minded, and can resist having our particular church denomination or tradition confused with others we feel are, in one way or another, misguided.

That said, I suggest it can help all of us to step back and look at the broad sweep of Protestant history. I have observed that Protestant churches have gravitated toward one of four major responses to civil government and its relationship to moral and civil law.

1. In countries that considered themselves Christian nations, state churches were established, and being a loyal citizen and being a Christian became almost identical.

2. Some churches have given more attention to defining the duty of Christian citizens to work at maintaining a Christian society with Christian values.

3. Some churches have focused more on a Christian's duty to live an individual moral life.

4. Some churches have paid attention to defining two distinct spheres of Christian concern, separating the kind of morality by which a Christian person is responsible to live from the kind of moral laws which a civil government can be held responsible to enforce.

I suggest these four ways of relating civil government to moral and civil law give us a basis for understanding how contemporary Protestant churches have reacted to the increasing acceptance of Marriage Equality. These four approaches to civil government do not neatly sort themselves out by denomination. Particular parishes and individuals may feel more at home with one way of dealing with civil and moral law while their tradition or denomination may have a different perspective. We Protestants may be loyal to our denominations; but we do like to make up our minds *for ourselves*.

As we look at our Protestant history with a wide-angle lens, we can see how these four different positions developed within our churches. The Lutheran churches in Western Europe, and later the Episcopal churches in Great Britain, developed their theological lives as state churches. The state sponsored these churches; and they have taken a role more or less supportive of the state. In England, the church so merged itself with society, that the country considered and still considers itself (officially, if not in practice) a Christian nation.

The Anabaptist churches in Europe, and later the Protestant and Puritan churches in the Americas, rejected the role of state church. Instead, they were moved by their faith in two opposite directions. There were Anabaptist and Radical Protestant groups whose faith led them to experiment with developing a Christian society. A small number of these groups took over the operation of individual cities, governing them by the dictates of their particular theology. Others developed Christian Utopian communities whose followers withdrew into separate enclaves. In both cases, the goal of these groups was to form a Christian government for their municipality or community.

Conversely, there were Anabaptist and Radical Protestant groups which had a more inward-looking and individual emphasis to their theology. Parts of the Pietistic movement in Europe and portions of the Revivalist movement in America, have both represented this impulse. In these churches, Christian faith was seen primarily as a force which transformed individual persons. These individual Christians could and did express their transformation by opposing the evils and injustices of society. As a rule, though, these churches were concerned with encouraging their members to exercise the duties of Christian citizenship. They did not consider it their mission to develop a Christian government or Christian civil society.

In the United States of America today, there are Protestant groups which act as though they have taken up the Christian Utopian dream of forming a Christian nation. Even though the United States has no state church, certainly no Christian state church, and has a constitution which defines our government in secular terms as neutral on matters of religion, these Protestant groups appear to have taken up the task of trying to turn The United States of America into *their version* of a Christian society.

The fourth strand of Protestantism, the Reformed or Presbyterian branch, is both deeply concerned with the morality of individual Christians and with holding its civil government morally responsible. The Reformed churches have historically taken a stand against forming a Christian society but have also taken great interest in the ethics of government. From John Calvin's interest in the civil government of Geneva Switzerland, to the interest of early American Presbyterians in forming a new government based on representative democracy, Presbyterians have believed human governments are called by God to be moral arbiters of society, but not religious arbiters.

Presbyterians share the same three fundamental gospel beliefs that were taught by Martin Luther, and that became the underpinning of the Reformation churches: grace alone, faith alone, and Scripture alone. Luther laid the foundation for the Reformation. In effect though, Calvin, the father of Reformed theology, was a second-generation Reformer. Calvin was born when Luther was 26. Calvin was just 8 years old when Luther nailed his 95 theses to the Wittenberg church door; just 10 years old when Luther published his seminal defense of the gospel in *Galatians*; and 11 years old when Luther published his groundbreaking call to reformation, *The Babylonian Captivity of the Church.* Calvin's own career as a reformer began with his publishing the first version of *The Institutes of the Christian Religion* at age 27, when Luther was already 56 years old. To be sure, Luther was still an active churchman; but he had made his mark on the Reformation by the time Calvin began his ministry.

Because of the theological foundation laid by Luther, Calvin had no need, in the words of the author of Hebrews, for "laying again a foundation of repentance from dead works and of faith toward God." Luther had proclaimed the Reformation's gospel message of: salvation by grace through faith; and all over Europe, Christian churches heard that gospel and joined the Reformation movement. Calvin was a teacher in a Reformation movement which had already begun.

As the young and growing Protestant churches with which Calvin dealt threw off political loyalty to the Pope, they found spiritual security by placing their confidence in Sacred Scripture. But they also began to wonder where to place their political loyalty. As noted, some states considered themselves Christian and sponsored Protestant churches which were loyal to the state. Other Protestant churches concentrated on working to form Christian societies and Christian municipalities.

Still other Protestants gave up on trying to perfect the human political world and focused only on the Christian transformation of individuals.

The Reformed and Presbyterian churches took a middle way which is relevant for American Protestants today. They focused on both Christian duty and governmental duty, and distinguished between the two. Reformed teachers held that Christian people receive the gift of God's grace, and by the power of that grace may live transformed lives ruled and constrained by Christ's love. And, while Reformed teachers had no such hopes for human, civil government, they expected civil government to pay attention to the two tables of God's moral law as written on the human conscience in the form of "natural law" (Romans 1:19 – 20). Reformed teachers understood the human awareness of "natural law" to be a pretty basic one, consisting of securing the freedom of all groups to worship God, maintaining an equitable justice for all citizens, and promoting social peace and stability. (You'll find this Reformed position spelled out and documented in the Study Paper.)

American citizens are historically interested in the actions of their government, and American Christians are no exception. The problem is that the Scriptures say many things about individual behavior, family behavior, community standards, good government and right worship. The challenge to conscientious Christians is to distinguish, among all these statements, those which are relevant to today's needs.

I invite all my fellow Protestants to continue reading Section 3 entitled, "With a Christ-Like Love." I believe this Study Paper provides a useful Protestant understanding of how both personal and civic morality relate to the contemporary question of Marriage Equality. It also demonstrates how a right understanding of the biblical message leads to a firm support for Marriage Equality.

If the message of this Study Paper resonates with you, I invite you to look again at the Couple's Letters and the Couple's Pamphlet in Section 1, and the Discussion Guide for Clergy in Section 2. The Couple's Letters and the Couple's Pamphlet in Section 1 take a more pastoral approach. The Guide for Clergy in Section 2 takes a more Christian Education approach to the challenges and joys of the love required by Christian Marriage within the context of Marriage Equality. All parts of this book are written from the perspective of Reformed biblical theology. After all, the Reformation and its theology are part of a heritage that, to differing degrees, we all share and can all draw from in guiding our decisions.

God bless each of you in your ministries

As we guide the church towards an acceptance of Marriage Equality and marriage inclusivity

The Rev. Steve R. Wigall, Th.M., Th.D.

December 2016

WITH A CHRIST-LIKE LOVE

A Study Paper providing a biblical and theological foundation for Civil Marriage Equality and Christian Marriage Inclusivity

I.   THE STUDY PAPER'S METHODS AND AIMS

This Study is a position paper which provides the scriptural and Reformed creedal foundation to *Preparing for Christian Marriage.* Its initial aim is to assist Presbyterian and Reformed pastors in their ministry to couples seeking Christian Marriage; however, all Protestant pastors who consult this Study Guide will find a consistent, biblical, and Reformation-based approach to understanding Christian Marriage. It addresses fundamental theological questions regarding Christian Marriage. And its careful, clear approach will allow its readers to confidently use it as a resource for helping couples discover a fuller meaning of Christian Marriage as a committed relationship between two people who strive to love each other for a lifetime "With a Christ-Like Love."

A biblical understanding of Christian Marriage is neither as immediately obvious, nor as easy to develop as it might seem. It requires identifying and questioning the interpretive assumptions we bring to

187

the task of understanding marriage. Marriage is such an essential and ingrained social custom, that as biblical interpreters, we need both to acknowledge the mores and traditions that shape our own cultural assumptions regarding marriage, and to identify the historical mores and traditions reflected in Scripture.

We may never remove every cultural bias from our personal interpretive lenses. We may never perfectly distinguish between what is essential to the Scripture's vision of marriage and what is cultural accretion. But this is what we are going to try to do. Only by doing our best to filter out human mores and traditions can we approach an understanding of Christian Marriage that reflects what God may intend marriage to be for today's People of God.

Clearly, we want to avoid being misled by faulty cultural assumptions. As we select and interpret Scripture passages, we want to be guided by true and helpful principles. These four Interpretive Principles express the assumptions which underlie the Reformed approach to Scripture. We will strive to follow them as guidelines

1. An honest reading of Scripture first tries to determine the text's original (historical and literary) meaning and then tries to determine its message for today.
   (BoC 5.010; 9.29; W 5.3002B)

2. The New Testament message provides the context for interpreting the Hebrew Scriptures and understands them as the Christian Old Testament.

   (BoC 6.039 – 6.042; 9.28)

3. The person and work of Christ provides the perspective for interpreting both the New and Old Testaments.

   (BoC 7.114; 8.11; 9.27; W 4.403b; 5.3001)

4. As Presbyterian and Reformed pastors and biblical interpreters, we look to "the Creeds of our church as authentic and reliable expositions of what Scripture leads us to believe and do."

(W 4.403c)

II MARRIAGE EQUALITY AND INCLUSIVITY: A REFORMED AND BIBLICAL POSITION

1. New Testament Marriage: Equality Replaces Procreation

Ephesians 5:31-33

> **Therefore a man shall leave his father and mother and hold fast to his wife, and the two shall become one flesh. This mystery is profound, and I am saying that it refers to Christ and the church. However, let each one of you love his wife as himself, and let the wife see that she respects her husband.**

Without question, Ephesians chapter five is the single most important passage for understanding the Christian view of marriage. The passage provides a Christian re-interpretation of marriage as it was originally explained in the Old Testament account of creation, specifically in Genesis, Chapter 2, verse 24. Note that in Genesis, marriage is cast within the drama of creation and given the role of procreation (see Genesis 1:27 – 28, and 3:21). In giving marriage a Christian reinterpretation, Ephesians shifts the meaning of marriage away from the archaic role of procreation, which marriage plays within creation, and gives it a new role within Christ's New Creation. We read in Ephesians, that in Christ, Christian Marriage takes on the new meaning of being a relationship between equals which requires both partners to learn to love each other with a Christ-like love.

The original Genesis explanation of marriage describes it as the way children from one generation establish the next generation of families. To achieve this goal, the Genesis-style marriage requires two people, a man and a woman, who play different roles (Genesis 2:24). The woman's role is to bear children and to stay with her husband so children are raised in a stable, intact family (Genesis 3:16). The man's role is to sweat as he works the ground to provide food to feed the family (Genesis 3:17 – 18). Genesis, the book of creation, describes family as an economically self-sustaining unit of pro-creation, in which a man and a woman join to give birth to and work to raise children. The Genesis-style family provides its society with a stable basis for a productive and growing population.

Ephesians shifts the context for understanding marriage and family from creation to New Creation. Instead of viewing family as a unit of procreation, family is re-envisioned in Christian terms as built around a marriage between two people who strive to love each other with a Christ-like love. Both husbands and wives are called to love in way that puts the other first (Ephesians 5:21). Wives are called to put their husbands first as the church does Christ (Ephesians 5:24). Husbands are called to put their wives first as Christ did the church when he gave his life to save and purify her (Ephesians 5:25 – 27).

Although the language of Ephesians calls husbands to love *as Christ loves the church*, and calls wives to love *as the church loves Christ*, it is same love to which both are called. Both marriage partners are called to a love that puts the other first. This is God's kind of love. We see and experience this love in Christ (II Corinthians 4:6; Ephesians 3:17 - 19). When the world sees this love shared in church within Christian fellowship, it experiences God's presence in our midst and knows we are Christ's Disciples (John 13:34 – 35). And it is this love Christian married couples are called to show each other.

Note that the Genesis description of marriage focuses on the procreative necessity for two partners who play different roles, that of man and woman. The Ephesians description focuses on the two partners becoming one and equal (Ephesians 5:31). In Genesis, where the function of marriage is procreation, the emphasis is on the need of partners to be different: specifically, to be male and female. In Ephesians, marriage functions to embody a Christ-like love, and the emphasis is on partners experiencing unity and equality.

Ephesians interprets marriage in the light of the Christian principle of equality in Christ. This principle is clearly articulated in Galatians 3:28: "There is neither Jew nor Greek, there is neither slave nor free, there is no male and female, for you are all one in Christ Jesus." Ephesians establishes the principle of equality primarily on faith in Christ, but then stretches its gaze further back to find an original basis in Genesis 2:24, which it quotes, stating: "a man shall leave his father and his mother and hold fast to his wife, and they shall become one flesh."

In Genesis, this phrase "one flesh," primarily refers to Adam's words, "Here is someone like me! She is part of my body, my own flesh and bones" (Genesis 2:23 CEV). The point made by the Genesis story is that the woman, unlike any of the other animals, qualifies as Adam's equal, a "suitable partner" for the man; so he need no longer "live alone" (Genesis 2:18 CEV). As the story continues, woman proves to be more than a suitable companion for man in their shared idyllic life in the garden. When the man and woman leave the garden, their equal partnership forms a "suitable" basis for stable families, able to produce the population growth needed for human societies to "be fruitful and multiply, increase greatly on the earth and multiply in it" (Genesis 9:7 CEV).

The Ephesians passage is remarkable for pronouncing that the purpose of Christian Marriage is deeper than supplying human companionship and more profound than providing society with an economically viable way to raise children. Certainly, it is important for the survival of society that humans have reliable companionship, and children are born and raised. But Christian Marriage has a higher purpose. Ephesians affirms that Christian Marriage calls both partners equally to exhibit a Christ-like love patterned after the love between Christ and the Church. The view that Christian Marriage teaches marriage partners to love as Christ loves fits perfectly into the New Testament description of the purpose of the Christian life.

Many metaphors are used by New Testament authors to describe the purpose of the Christian life; but the following three passages, taken together, express the thrust of New Testament message.

1. Romans 8:29 says that God works in the lives of people to conform them to the image of God's Son.

2. II Corinthians 3:18 says that the Lord Jesus Christ works in the lives of God's people imparting an ever-increasing glory to them while transforming them into God's image.

3. 1 John 3:2 says that the transformation of God's People will not be complete until Christ returns at the end of the age. Christ will complete transforming God's people at that time, and they will find they have been changed to be like Christ.

God's plan for human life is Christ-likeness; and Christian Marriage fits into God's plan by teaching people to love with a Christ-like kind of love. Those who accept Christian Marriage are schooled in an essential characteristic of God's love. Christian Marriage teaches the crucial lesson of loving faithfully.

Throughout Scripture, God is described as faithful. When God appears face-to-face with Moses, God declares his character with the words, "The Lord, the Lord, a God merciful and gracious, slow to anger, and abounding in steadfast love and faithfulness," (Exodus 34:6). The Psalms repeatedly praise God's faithfulness. For example, "Your steadfast love, O LORD, extends to the heavens, your faithfulness to the clouds." (Psalms 36:5). And the Prophet Jeremiah writes, "The steadfast love of the Lord never ceases; his mercies never come to an end; they are new every morning; great is your faithfulness." (Lamentations 3:22 – 23).

The New Testament repeats the same message: God is faithful. Christians are particularly encouraged to trust God to sustain them, because "God is <u>faithful</u>" (I Corinthians 1:9 - 10). Christians not only know that God who is faithful includes them in Christ's saving fellowship, but know God is also "a <u>faithful</u> creator" (I Peter 4:9).

Learning to love with a love that is faithful, like God's love is faithful, is essential to Christian Marriage. This is the bottom line. The commitment to love your partner faithfully for a lifetime is the primary constituent of Christian Marriage.

It is important, as pastors and teachers of the Christian faith, that we uphold the moral and spiritual integrity of Christian Marriage. To do that, we need to be sure we have identified from our study of Scripture the moral and spiritual values which are central to Christian Marriage. This means we need to realize that our understanding of Christian Marriage must grow beyond seeing it only in the context of creation, with the sole purpose of procreation. Because the Genesis understanding of marriage focuses on the mandate to give birth to and raise children, it restricted marriage to being an instrument of procreation. Now seen in the light of the New Testament, Christian Marriage increasingly finds its meaning in the New Creation mandate to embody the faithfulness of Christ-like love. We need to realize, that to uphold the integrity of Christian Marriage, we are called to maintain the sacredness of making a life-long promise to love one partner faithfully.

Reformed thinking bases its understanding of every aspect of Christian life, including Christian ethics, on the witness of Scripture. This study follows a Reformed approach to the ethics of Christian Marriage by basing its conclusions on Scripture. It is important to say that Reformed thinking does not simply repeat the scriptural interpretation of former Reformed teachers. Neither does it simply quote every Scripture passage that speaks to a topic and summarize the collective message. Instead, Reformed thinking is based on closely following a Reformed approach to understanding Scripture. For the purpose of this discussion of Christian Marriage, we're going to follow the description of the Reformed approach to Scripture as it is succinctly summarized by the four Interpretive Principles listed towards the beginning of this essay. We're now going to review these four Principles and examine how each one is used in this study.

<u>Interpretive Principle One</u>: An honest reading of Scripture first tries to determine the text's original (historical and literary) meaning and then tries to determine its message for today.

In keeping with that principle, we take three foundational Scripture texts that describe marriage and look for their original intent or meaning. We examine Genesis 2:24, which defines marriage. We examine the creation stories in Genesis chapters 1 through 10, which provide a context for this definition. And we examine Ephesians 5:31 – 33 where the Genesis definition is quoted and reinterpreted in Christian terms. In attempting to state the original meaning of these texts, we interpret each one as part of a literary composition (i.e. a biblical *book*). It might have been possible to deconstruct these three texts to differentiate and distinguish between their original sources. It might have been possible to examine Genesis, in particular, as an historical record and comment on its historicity, or lack thereof. However, this study proceeds on the assumption that Scripture does not contain history in the modern sense of the term: a written, fact-based record of events. Instead, this study chooses to pursue the "original meaning" of scriptural texts in terms of their literary or exegetical meaning within the work of literature, or biblical book, in which they are found.

For example, an honest interpretation of the definition of marriage, found in Genesis chapter two, realizes the text does not address the situation of Adam and Eve. This definition of marriage occurs early in the creation narrative, and is spoken either by Adam as he describes his relationship with Eve, or by the Genesis narrator as a comment on Adam's relationship with Eve. However, neither Adam nor Eve have *a father and mother* whom they must *leave* in order to *get married*, thus joining their two lives in marriage, and making them *like one*. Because these words are spoken as though they were a description of the first constituted marriage, they take on particular weight and authority within the context of Genesis.

Among the characters within the arc of the creation narratives, this definition of marriage is most likely addressed to the children of Noah (see Genesis 9) who were the descendants of the children of Adam (see Genesis 5). To these early families fell the responsibility to begin and spread human civilization by multiplying and populating the earth (Genesis 9:7). However, according to Genesis 6:5, their initial efforts at civilization-building were far from a success. They very much needed instructions for building the kind of strong family units on which a stable human civilization could be based. These families needed to be taught how to construct intact and thriving families which would ensure a successful context for procreation, and in turn, ensure successive generations of families would be there to provide the reliably growing population needed by an expanding human civilization.

The lesson being taught to a young and growing human civilization is that it would need procreation to take place within family units made secure by the commitment and loyalty of family members to each other. We can even imagine how this important first definition of marriage might have been passed on to us from the earliest human families. Family elders might have related the story to their children, who might well have communicated it to generation after generation of their descendants, until today the story belongs to all of us who claim the Hebrew Bible as Scripture. From the beginning, the crown jewel of family life has been the loyal commitment of its members to each other. For Christian Marriage, it is the same.

Interpretive Principle Two: The New Testament message provides the context for interpreting the Hebrew Scriptures, and understands them as the Christian Old Testament.

Our approach to understanding the Genesis passages has been based on the Reformed principle that the Hebrew Bible is the Christian Old Testament. As Reformed Christians, we do not dismiss the books the Hebrew Bible as irrelevant to our faith; nor do we discount them as containing an outmoded message made obsolete by Christ. Reformed Christians receive the Hebrew Bible as a genuine word from God that testifies to the covenant of Grace, teaches salvation by faith, and points towards Christ.

When we accept the book of Genesis as part of the Christian Old Testament, we receive its definition of marriage as Scripture, and as a word from God which contains an important teaching about marriage. But we also read the Genesis definition of marriage by examining how it points to Christ. How the Genesis definition of marriage points to Christ is made clear in Ephesians 5:32 – 33. Ephesians quotes the Genesis passage, lifting out its underlying theme of unity and equality, and bringing that latent theme to the fore as the centerpiece of the Christian reinterpretation of Marriage.

Because Reformed Christians accept the Genesis definition of marriage as Scripture, we hold that Christian Marriage *may consist of* a procreative relationship between one man and one woman. We hold that this kind of faithful, procreative relationship can be a joyful and meaningful expression of God's intention for marriage. The New Testament definition of Marriage cannot nullify the Old Testament definition. It can only complete and fulfill it (see Matthew 5:17).

Reformed Christians hold that giving birth to and raising children is a profound context for learning to love and can be an important and treasured component of marriage. However, Reformed Christians do not hold procreation to be the essence of Christian Marriage. A procreative definition of marriage provides neither a sufficient nor a relevant understanding of marriage in its New Testament context. In the New Testament, Christian Marriage is a faithful, Christ-like love between two equal partners.

Defining marriage as a faithful, procreative relationship between one man and one woman is clearly consistent with the terms of the Genesis definition. However, the Genesis definition is too restricted and *insubstantial* (lacking in substance) to uphold the moral and spiritual integrity of Christian Marriage. Christian Marriage, as described in the New Testament (specifically in Ephesians), does not abandon, but rises beyond the Genesis definition, which would limit marriage to being merely a procreative union. In order for Christian Marriage to realize its full meaning, it needs to be understood as a loving and committed relationship between two persons who treat each other as equals, and who together embody the faithfulness of Christ-like love.

Interpretive Principle Three: The person and work of Christ provides the perspective for interpreting both the New and Old Testaments.

Reformed Christians view the Old Testament through the interpretative lens of the person and work of Christ. This is exactly the way in which Ephesians 5:31 – 33 interprets Genesis 2:24. In this passage, the author of Ephesians identifies the theme of "oneness in Christ" as the motif around which he builds the understanding of Christian Marriage. Oneness is an important theme for the Apostle Paul. The apostle both describes Christians as *one* with Christ (Romans 6:5; 7:4); and tells Christians to express their *oneness* in Christ through their relationships with each other (e.g. Galatians 3:28; Philippians 1:27).

Having chosen the Pauline theme of *oneness* in Christ to define Christian Marriage, the author of Ephesians turns to the Old Testament for a passage on which he can base a Christian reinterpretation of Marriage. He looks to the Genesis definition of marriage, where he finds support for the theme he has chosen to use as a basis for understanding Christian Marriage: *oneness*. The New Testament describes *oneness* in Christ using such words as: united, joined, one, one spirit, one mind, and one body. Genesis describes the *oneness* that exists within the marriage bond by using the phrase, "one flesh." The Hebrew phrase usually translated as "one flesh" is used in Genesis and in Ephesians to carry several meanings. It refers to being *like* or *kin to* another person, to being *joined in partnership with* another person to create a new family, and to a relationship of equality in which two people see and treat each other, equally, *as one person.*

Reformed Christians accept the original message of Genesis regarding marriage is a part of the Hebrew Bible, and therefore, God's word to us. We accept that procreation can be a sacred and God-blessed part of a marriage relationship. But like the author of the Book of Ephesians, Reformed Christians also find in Genesis a more profound statement about marriage that points towards the life and work of Christ. This more profound understanding comes from seeing marriage as an expression of the *oneness* which lies at the heart of Christ's work in this world. Reformed Christians believe Christ is at work in human lives to *unite* us with himself, and to call us to live *as one* with fellow Christians. So the heart, the meaning, and the challenge of Christian Marriage is for two people to embody and express a shared and faithful relationship of *oneness* both with Christ and with each other.

2.   Christian Marriage Is a Moral Relationship Defined by Sexual Faithfulness and the Rejection of Lust.

There are other Scripture passages pertaining to marriage we will need to examine and include in a biblical view of Christian Marriage. Some passages are contained in Wisdom literature and offer practical advice about married life. These we will discuss in section two of this book, entitled, "A Discussion Guide for Clergy". Other passages lay down ethical prohibitions regarding marriage. To rightly understand these prohibitions or laws, we will adhere to the fourth Interpretive Principle which tells us to follow the teaching of the Reformed Creeds when construing the meaning of law in Scripture.

Interpretive Principle Four: As Presbyterian and Reformed pastors and biblical interpreters, we look to "the confessions of our church as authentic and reliable expositions of what Scripture leads us to believe and do."

This may be the most important of the Reformed principles for developing a biblical understanding of Christian Marriage. It directs us to follow the guidance of the Reformed Creeds when reading and interpreting Scripture. This is important because from the Creeds, we learn Scripture presents us with three kinds of ethical statements, or laws. The Westminster Confession of Faith names these three kinds of laws as the moral, the ceremonial, and the judicial (BoC. 6.103 – 104). The point is each kind of scriptural law needs to be interpreted and understood on its own terms because each has a distinct function. The Westminster Confession of Faith describes the function of the moral law when it states it is "written in two tables; the first four commandments containing our duty toward God, and the other six our duty to man" (BoC, 6.102). The Second Helvetic Confession also names the three kinds of scriptural law and describes the function of ceremonial and judicial law (BoC, 5.081):

> For the sake of clarity, we distinguish the moral law which is contained in the Decalogue or two Tables and is expounded in the books of Moses, the ceremonial law which determines the ceremonies and worship of God, and the judicial law which is concerned with political and domestic matters.

Calvin further expounds on the importance of distinguishing between these three kinds of scriptural law (John Calvin, Institutes of the Christian Religion, Book IV, Chapter 20, Section 15):

> We must attend to the well-known division which distributes the whole law of God, as promulgated by Moses, into the moral, the ceremonial, and the judicial law, and we must attend to each of these parts, in order to understand how far they do, or do not, pertain to us.

Toward the end of this section, Calvin strongly warns against confusing the Scripture's moral law with either the ceremonial or the judicial law. He writes, "Let no one be moved by the thought that the judicial and ceremonial laws relate to morals" (Calvin, Book IV, Chapter 20, Section 15).

To rightly develop a Reformed biblical understanding of Christian Marriage, as we would when developing any Christian moral position, we need to base our conclusions firmly on those scriptural passages which contain moral law and intend to give moral guidance. The Westminster Confession of Faith clearly defines moral law when it states this: "this law, commonly called moral, God was pleased to give to the people of Israel" and it "was delivered by God upon Mount Sinai in ten commandments" (BoC, 6.102 – 6.103).

The testimony of early Reformed theology, including the witness of the Reformed Creeds, clearly warns us not to add any of our own rules to "the Decalogue or two Tables as expounded in the books of Moses" (BoC 5.081). However, when it comes to defining Christian Marriage, we may easily be drawn to add a view that reflects our cultural and religious traditions: we may decide to define marriage as a relationship between one man and one woman. This view has longstanding support in Western Civilization's cultural and religious traditions.

It is important for us to realize, however, the Reformed Creeds warn against the danger of supporting culturally biased moral rules "which have no other warrant than the invention and opinion of man" (BoC 3.14); or those based "on the traditions of men" (BoC 4.091). We may be convinced the definition of marriage which restricts it to a relationship between one man and one woman actually promotes social and religious decency (BoC 6.087). But the Lord has "forbidden us to add or to take away anything from this law" (BoC 5.082). The most important Reformed principle to grasp when trying to understand the Christian view of marriage is that we can only base Christian moral convictions on moral law which we believe God only gives us in and through The Ten Commandments.

This means, in part, that we need to be able to identify which laws in Scripture are ceremonial so we can avoid using them as a basis for understanding marriage. To be clear, ceremonial law consists of those rules in Scripture governing personal and communal worship life. In the Old Testament, ceremonial law includes the rules that direct personal and communal sacrifices, as well as the celebration of holy days. Ceremonial law also contains rules defining what is clean and unclean and how to fulfil the Nazarite vows. All of these ceremonial laws play an important role in defining Israel's worship life.

We can also find examples of ceremonial law in the New Testament. The rule directing women to cover their hair in church, and the rule directing the Corinthians to share food equally during their community Lord's Supper are both ceremonial law. Ceremonial law in either Testament prescribes worship behavior. Old Testament ceremonial law may state obedience to it is a condition of human holiness. However, ceremonial law describes only the worship duties of a particular community – the Jewish community in the Old Testament; or the local church community in the New Testament. In both cases, it is helpful to remember the warning of Calvin that we must not think that "ceremonial laws relate to morals" (Calvin, Book IV, Chapter 20, Section 15).

We also want to avoid using judicial law as a basis for understanding Christian Marriage. For that reason, we need to be clear what judicial law is. Distinguishing judicial law from genuine moral law may present a problem. Judicial law may seem to command legitimately moral behavior, and interdict legitimately immoral behavior; but that is not the case. Moral law consists of only the Decalogue or Ten Commandments. These laws, given by God, apply to all people in all circumstances and all social conditions. The essential quality of judicial law is that it is meant to apply strictly to the circumstances of the ruler being discussed or the conditions of the society being addressed.

For example, in the Old Testament, God gives political guidance to the people of Israel for setting up their government. That guidance takes the form of specific rules describing how the nation is to conduct its business. God also gives social guidance to the people of Israel for shaping their community life. That guidance takes the form of specific rules describing how the people are to behave and not behave. The political and social guidance which God gives Israel is made up of judicial law intended *just for them.* Because the Ten Commandments are moral law, they apply to everyone.

The universal applicability of Old Testament judicial law was much debated during the early Reformation period. There were radical religious groups which taught Christians should strive to apply Israel's political and social laws to their local city or state government. Calvin makes it clear, as do the Reformed Creeds, that this is misguided. The political and social laws of Israel are meant by God to apply to Israel alone and not to any other nation or society. In Calvin, we read,

> The Lord did not deliver it [judicial law] by the hand of Moses to be promulgated in all countries, and to be everywhere enforced; but having taken the Jewish nation under his special care, patronage, and guardianship, he was pleased to be specially its legislator, and as became a wise legislator, he had special regard to it in enacting laws (Calvin, Book IV, Chapter 20, Section 16).

The Westminster Confession makes the same point.

> To them [the people of Israel] also, as a body politic, he [God)] gave sundry judicial laws, which expired together with the state of that people, not obliging any other, now, further than the general equity thereof may require (BoC 6.104).

It is important for our understanding of Christian Marriage that we have discussed the three-fold division of law in Reformed thought because Christian Marriage is at least a threefold undertaking. Christian Marriage is, in part, a ceremonial event which is customarily consecrated by a service of worship. However, Christian Marriage cannot be defined by any of the worship services which celebrate it. It is, in part, a judicial event regulated by civil law which defines it as a social contract between two consenting individuals. However, Christian Marriage cannot be reduced to a statute of state contract law.

It is essential to a right understanding of Christian Marriage to realize it is, by nature, a moral event with a spiritual identity defined and safeguarded by two of the Ten Commandments. The moral definition of marriage finds its heart in the command which says in effect: Be faithful to one sexual partner (Exodus 20:14). The marriage relationship is further defined and strengthened by the moral command which says in effect: Do not treat your marriage partner as an object of lust to be possessed or used (Exodus 20:17). Because marriage is a moral question, any Christian definition of marriage needs to be based on the Ten Commandments, and needs to reject any attempt to add other commands or restrictions to this definition.

As stated earlier in this study, a Christian Marriage may legitimately be between one man and one woman. But, as we have also seen, there is no biblical basis for stating a Christian Marriage *must be* between one man and one woman. What a Christian Marriage must be is a relationship between two people who are sexually faithful to each other and who refuse to view or treat each other as objects to be owned. In addition, as we previously discussed, a New Testament view of Christian Marriage sees it as a love relationship between two people who strive both to treat each other as equals and to grow towards *oneness* with Christ and with each other. The Reformed Creeds would have us state at this point that no other rules or laws must be added or taken away from this biblical definition.

3. The Guidance of the Reformed Creeds Regarding Civil Marriage

Although Christian Marriage is a spiritual and moral reality, in all Western cultures, marriage is also a legal status which society bestows on couples. Legally constituted or civil marriage grants qualified couples the rights and privileges coming from being treated as one person for the purposes of legal and financial transactions. We can say Christian Marriage is the spiritual union of two lives, but we also need to be aware civil marriage is a legally recognized contract between two people who essentially go into business together by formally committing themselves to join in a lifelong, legal partnership.

In Genesis, we read that marriage provided early human society with stable families where children were born and raised, and work was accomplished. Both ancient and modern societies need the kind of growing population and strong work force which families can provide. For that reason, society has an ongoing interest in safeguarding the legal and financial status of families.

It is important to realize however, civil law has no reason to reflect the values of Christian Marriage. If Christian Marriage were only a spiritual or moral matter, like Baptism or Confirmation, civil law would have no reason to recognize it at all. Marriage only gains status in civil law because it fulfills the two essential social functions described in Genesis:

1) To provide society with a stable means of giving birth to and raising children

And:

2) To provide society with a stable supply of motivated workers

The Church sees the role of marriage differently. It teaches that Christian Marriage is a sexually faithful relationship between two people who promise to love each other for a lifetime. The Church teaches these couples to embrace sexual fidelity as a context for learning how to love another person with the faithfulness of God's love. The Church further teaches married individuals not to reduce their partner to an object of lust or to treat their partner as a possession.

The Reformed tradition has recognized from its inception that Christians participate in society, and may be able to take a role in shaping its laws. The question is, "What kind of civil marriage laws would be appropriate for Reformed Christians to support?" As we have demonstrated, Reformed Christians make decisions (such as deciding the nature of marriage), by studying the message of Scripture. However, while Scripture gives substantial guidance regarding individual and community behavior, it gives very little direct guidance regarding governmental behavior and lawmaking.

Here is where Reformed Christians can take advantage of their confessional heritage. The Reformed Creeds give government officials (or magistrates) the responsibility to enact and enforce *the right kind of* civil laws. The Second Helvetic Confession states the magistrate's duty is to "govern the people entrusted to him by God with good laws according to the Word of God" (BoC 5.253). The Westminster Confession of Faith describes these "good laws" which the civil magistrate has a duty to enforce, as being of two general types (BoC 6.129).

> It is the duty of civil magistrates to protect the church of our common Lord, without giving the preference to any denomination of Christians above the rest . . . .

And,

> It is the duty of civil magistrates to protect the person and good name of all their people, in such an effectual manner as that no person be suffered, either upon pretense of religion or infidelity, to offer any indignity, violence, abuse, or injury to any other person whatsoever . . . .

Briefly stated then, the function of civil law is to protect the worship of God, and maintain the rule of justice for all citizens. From the multicultural perspective of modern society, Westminster might not seem magnanimous when it extends civil protection only to *Christian* denominations. Westminster does not admit that Jewish synagogues or other religious houses of worship deserve civil protection because they, too, promote the worship of God. Still, for Westminster's historical time frame, it goes a long way towards establishing the *spirit of equity* and fair treatment among religions.

Consider that neither the churches of the Reformation, nor Calvin himself, were always shining examples of toleration towards Christians with whom they differed. Most of the Protestant denominations involved in the founding of the American colonies were not enthusiastic about religious freedom for *rival* Christian denominations. And, in recent times, the Protestants of Northern Ireland struggled, sometimes violently, against extending toleration and equality for Catholic Christians. In this context, it is worthy of note that Westminster avoids insisting all Christians agree; and it takes the step of giving civil governments the responsibility to ensure religious freedom for every Christian denomination despite their disagreements.

The two kinds of "good laws" described in The Westminster Confession, those safeguarding the worship of God, and those upholding the rule of justice, parallel the two areas of concern for civil magistrates described by Calvin in Institutes, Book IV, Chapter 20: Civil Gov-ernment. There Calvin writes that civil magistrates are called to maintain laws upholding the moral laws' two tables: the worship of God, and justice in society. A "concern for both tables of the law," writes Calvin in section 9 of this chapter, is to guide how civil magistrates govern. In section 15, Calvin explains that although magistrates may be guided by the moral law's two tables, they are not to enforce statutes mimicking them. Instead, "every nation is left free to make such laws as it foresees is profitable for itself."

Despite the freedom which Calvin says God gives each nation to make civil laws fitting its needs, Calvin still teaches all civil law should broadly follow "the moral law [which] is contained under two heads, one of which simply commands us to worship God with pure faith and piety, the other, to embrace men with sincere affection" (Calvin, Book IV, Chapter 20, Section 15). Calvin concludes his discussion of civil law in section 16 of Chapter 20 by stating there is a good reason civil law follows the broad contours of "the moral law of God, delivered by God to Moses." According to Calvin, this is because moral law "is an expression of natural law, at once [originally] written on the human heart, and a reflection of equity." He means that human civil law should strive to enforce the principle of equity found in God's moral law, because even if equity is imperfectly present in human minds, it remains an indelible part of human consciousness.

Calvin teaches that the human awareness of God's moral law is expressed in civil law through a concern for justice and fairness: or equity. He writes, "equity alone must be the goal and rule and limit of all [human] laws" (Calvin, Book IV, Chapter 20, Section 16). We do not refer to Calvin in this study because Calvin's teaching has equal standing with the Reformed Creeds; Calvin has a place in this study because the Reformed Creeds both reflect Calvin's interest in civil law and follow much of his fundamental teaching on the subject.

For example, Calvin begins his definition of civil law with the idea that it reflects the dual concerns of the moral law's two tables – promoting both the worship of God and justice for all people. The Westminster Confession follows Calvin by stating civil law has this same dual duty. However, as Calvin finishes his definition of civil law in section 16, of chapter 20, Book IV, before going on to discuss the right relationship of Christians to civil law in sections 17 – 31, he shifts from a dual to a unitary understanding of civil law, explaining that its essence is based on innate human moral awareness, or "that conscience which God has engraved on the minds of men." This moral awareness, writes Calvin, is fundamentally an expression of the principle of equity (Calvin, Book IV, Chapter 20, Section 16). It is the theme of equity or justice on which the remainder of the Reformed creeds base their definition of civil law.

The Scots Confession declares God intends human government to enforce justice in the form of the "defense of good men, and the punishment of all evildoers." In the Scots Confession, it makes clear that the kind of civil justice which God ordains is not to be the privilege of the rich and powerful. Civil justice properly means securing "the good and well-being of all men" (BoC 3.24).

The Second Helvetic Confession also states the duty of civil law is to maintain justice for all people. Justice in the Helvetic Confession means protecting the weak, and punishing those who prey on them. The confession states, "Let him [the magistrate] protect widows, orphans, and the afflicted. Let him punish and even banish criminals, imposters, and barbarians. For he does not bear the sword in vain" (BoC 5.254). However, The Second Helvetic Confession extends the definition of justice beyond its impact on the individual to include communal or social justice which it describes as peace. It states, "The chief duty of the magistrate is to secure and preserve peace and public tranquility. (BoC 5.253).

The Declaration of Barmen is a modern Creed that also defines justice as both an individual and a societal matter. It states, "Scripture tells us that, in the as yet unredeemed world in which the church also exists, the State has by divine appointment the task of providing for justice and peace" (BoC 8.22).

This is the conclusion then. The Reformed Creeds guide citizens and magistrates to support civil laws enforcing equal justice before the law for all individuals and securing the peace of society. Reformed Christians are called to believe "good law" regarding marriage should follow this guidance. We are also called to follow this guidance in deciding the kind of civil marriage laws to support. Reformed Christians are called to support the kind of marriage law that meets 1) the demands of justice by giving all people seeking marriage equal treatment before the law, and 2) ensures the peace of society at large. In the next section, we will see how Marriage Equality meets both of these goals.

III.   SOCIETY NEEDS MARRIAGE LAW ADMINISTERING IN-
DIVIDUAL JUSTICE AND ESTABLISHING SOCIETAL PEACE.

1.   Examining the social objections to same-sex marriage demonstrates how well Marriage Equality fits the need of civil law to promote social justice and the peace (i.e. the wellbeing) of society.

This study has demonstrated a Reformed understanding of Scripture leads to the support of Marriage Equality. We now turn to address the social objections to same-sex marriage that have shaped much of today's societal and religious debate. For example:

1)   It has been objected the gay lifestyle is essentially promiscuous and, consequently, morally inconsistent with marriage.

I've stated this objection in the way I most often hear it. In fact though, there is no "gay lifestyle." It might be argued the gay rights movement of the 1960's emphasized the identity and values of the gay community as opposed to the identity and values of the straight community. I suggest the early gay rights movement rightly had a strong investment in solidifying and energizing the gay community. That earlier movement identified the gay community as sharing common values and interests. While there was and is a gay community in the sense gay citizens share a common interest in gaining political and social freedoms; there is no gay community defined by shared gay values or a gay lifestyle.

The contemporary LGBTQ movement is a gay community united by a common interest in achieving political freedom and social dignity. But the LGBTQ movement has developed a strong investment in recognizing the diversity of lifestyles among gay citizens, a diversity as wide and complex as American society as a whole. And the LGBTQ movement has rightly embraced the interests of gay citizens to fully participate in society. Since gay citizens are the children and family members of straight citizens, the society as a whole has a strong interest in fully acknowledging and incorporating its gay members. Today, the notion there is an identifiable gay lifestyle tends to be a misconception promoted by anti-gay voices, who are intent on characterizing gay people as sexually promiscuous. In reality, sexual promiscuity can be found among people of all sexual orientations.

But perhaps the best answer to this objection comes from the words of the apostle Paul. In chapter seven of his first letter to Christians at Corinth, Paul discusses very plainly the advantages of marriage. He suggests marriage should be universally available because it is the best way to curb the sexual passion which unbridled leads to promiscuity (I Corinthians 7:2, 9). Paul's endorsement of marriage constitutes good advice for society. If codified in civil law, equal access to marriage would limit promiscuity, and promote the peace and stability of the whole social structure.

Civil society has the right to be concerned about the stability of families and to take action preventing widespread sexual promiscuity. To encourage stable families, the state would do well to act on the Apostle Paul's advice that marriage is the best means of curbing promiscuous behavior. The state would be strengthened by granting all its sexually active citizens access to marriage. As long as these citizens are old enough to make legally binding decisions for themselves, the state gains in stability by making civil marriage widely available.

Giving all couples equal access to marriage would clearly promote fairness and justice. It would minimize sexual promiscuity by maximizing the number of sexually committed married couples. Consequently, it would also promote the peace and stability of society. Marriage equality safeguards both social justice and social peace. By favoring laws encouraging Marriage Equality, Christians reaffirm our belief that the function of civil law is to uphold justice and peace. By standing for Marriage Equality, we announce our Scripture-based conviction that the moral boundary defining marriage isn't heterosexual love. Our conviction is that marriage is morally defined by the commitment of two people to love each other faithfully for a lifetime.

2)   It has been objected that society finds many gay behaviors offensive, and that it risks legitimating these offensive behaviors by allowing gays to marry. It is possible many individuals hold their fellow gay citizens guilty of offensive behavior. Behaviors such as the caricature of femininity expressed in drag, effeminate behavior in men, butch behavior in women, are all behaviors which may be offensive to some individuals. I should add, at this point, that gender role stereotyping oppresses people of all sexual orientations. Every man and every woman should be free to express their masculinity or femininity in ways that feel authentic to them. And yet we know that gender role norms are often straightjackets which individuals need to deconstruct and restructure to fit their personal inclinations. At this point, what I want to emphasize, though, is the impact of marginalization.

We should consider the question of whether these behaviors are intrinsic to marginalization or intrinsic to being gay. We should also consider the question of the freedom which all citizens should have to express themselves as they see fit as long as no one else is harmed. But the most important question may be, "How does society socialize its gay citizens?" Any group of people who are marginalized by society in a way that hinders their free socialization, will develop unique behaviors to define and express themselves. Some of the marginalized group's behaviors may cause them to stand out as different. Some of these behaviors may also be considered offensive. All social outcasts exhibit behaviors which their society considers offensive.

There's actually an easy and obvious way to change the undesirable behavior of any marginalized people. Stop marginalizing them! Social inclusion is one of most powerful methods of shaping and "homogenizing" any group's behavior. Nothing creates behavioral conformity like being accepted into society's inner circles. Those people who want to withhold marriage from gay couples because they judge gay behavior is offensive are simply thinking backwards. Family and marriage are firmly at the center of our social experience. We learn to define ourselves there and we learn our basic values and behavior patterns there. Extend the right of marriage to gay couples and you can guarantee they will end up behaving just like every other *good ol' American* married couple.

It cannot be stated too often that the interests of justice and fairness are served by extending the right of marriage to all gay citizens. But it is also in the interests of the peace and wellbeing of society to limit the social conflict which may arise from prejudice against the behavior of marginalized gay citizens. Society can begin to limit any behavior of gay couples which may be judged offensive by realizing these behaviors are created in large part by restricting gay involvement in the socializing power of marriage. Law that supports Marriage Equality can only have the effect of diminishing the degree to which gay couples behave in any way that differs from or is objectionable to their fellow citizens.

3)   Another objection to legalizing gay marriage suggests it would be offensive to do anything to encourage the public display of affection (PDA) by gay couples. The suggestion is that the PDA of gay couples offends public decency. It is even suggested that it potentially corrupts the morals of impressionable young people.

In fact, when the PDA of gay couples is objected to, a more complicated issue arises. It is easiest to understand this kind of objection as a result of developmental psychology and not as a matter of either morality or socialization. Prior to puberty, most young people find all kinds of public kissing, hugging, and affectionate behavior to be objectionable (or yucky). During adolescence, the human brain is bathed in hormones giving us a whole new perspective on affectionate touch. The human attitude towards PDA changes during puberty from negatively judging it (as yucky), to regarding it as positive or even heart-warming.

However, this adolescent transition has a variable component – a slightly unpredictable sexual polarity. Most adults report developing a personal interest in affectionate touch between themselves and a person of the opposite sex. However, a significant minority of adults report developing a personal interest in affectionate touch between themselves and a person of the same sex.

If we might agree that physical affection makes a positive contribution to human well being, perhaps we could also agree that society as a whole benefits from the adult acceptance of *some degree* of PDA. However, there are two aspects of PDA about which we will not all agree. Although we all share the experience of adolescence, we don't all emerge from it with the same reaction to receiving affectionate touch from the opposite sex or from the same sex. Neither do we all agree about *how much intimate touch* is acceptable in public.

Biblical morality does not help define how much public intimacy is acceptable; neither does adolescence create human agreement on the question. However, we are not left without guidance. PDA can easily be regulated just like other aspects of our social lives. We all avoid needless social offence simply by trying to be polite. In different social contexts, in different locations, and among different groups, being polite allows couples to express a greater degree of affection while sometimes it requires them to express less.

PDA is not an issue unique to gay couples. I've been young, been part of a young couple, and today enjoy observing the happiness of young couples. And I've noticed young couples are more inclined to greater indulgence in PDA than middle-aged and older couples. What happened to all of us who were once young couples happens to all other young couples as they grow up. We are all socialized to share our affection for each other in more private places or in public places where physical affection is accepted – like at a family gathering, or a private booth at a romantic restaurant, or (if we are young enough) at a local lovers' lane.

Socialization is a powerful force that effectively motivates couples to limit displaying affection for each other to places where it won't cause offence. Most gay couples already know how to be polite and discreet about PDA. And there is every reason to expect that the more gay couples are brought into the mainstream of public life by giving public acceptance to same-sex marriages, the more same-sex couples will follow the agreed upon rules for polite behavior all other couples follow.

4)   There is a misguided objection which claims the sexual activity of gay couples causes the spread of AIDS; and that Marriage Equality, which would legitimize gay sexual unions, would also increase the spread of AIDS and other terrible sexually transmitted diseases (STDs).

This objection is both factually misguided and easy to address. We now know AIDS is not a respecter of sexual orientation, (or of age or social class). In America, many gay men have been its victim, but the spread of STD's is not linked to sexual orientation. It is particularly linked to a sexual psychopathology indifferent to the welfare of sexual partners.

AIDS may also be accidently contracted and spread by the arrogant individual who believes they cannot get it. Citizens who think only "other people" contract AIDS, and do not protect themselves from it, are a danger to all their sexual partners. The use of condoms goes a long way to protect the health of sexually active citizens. But, the most effective protection of sexual health is a sexually faithful marriage. Although marriage is not foolproof protection, simply encouraging couples to be in sexually faithful relationships significantly limits the spread of all STD's. Marriage laws that encourage every sexually active couple, gay and straight, to enter faithfully into the contract of marriage can only have the outcome of limiting STD infection rates in the general population. Marriage equality before the law bolsters the peace and wellbeing of society, because by limiting disease, it promotes public health.

5)   Perhaps the most tragic objection to Marriage Equality is the claim that same-sex marriage is a threat to family life. When families see a gay son or daughter as a threat, morally or socially, they are at best,

likely to show their child and same-sex partner a cold or be-grudging tolerance, and at worst, expel them from the family circle.

The truth is that every attempt to ban same-sex marriage is a direct attack on the life of the American family. I know of individuals and groups who oppose Marriage Equality, who I am sure believe they are trying to protect American families. But I have to ask myself, "Where do they think young gay men and gay women come from: the cabbage patch?" They are our sons and our daughters. They are children of American families. I have to believe their parents treasure them and did their best to raise them in the loving embrace of a caring family. I know no family is perfect, and many children grow up with painful experiences of family life. But I also observe it is nearly impossible to grow up in The United States of America without being surrounded by the idea of family.

No matter how troubled the early family experience of any American citizen, they are exposed to family life everywhere they look: on TV, in public school, in churches, and among neighborhood friends. In America, we raise our children to grow up with dreams of getting married and starting a family. We simply don't raise our children to dream of growing up and living alone. Our children don't aspire to lives of faithless promiscuity or lives of single celibacy. They may have experiences leading them to choose one of these two lifestyles. But neither celibacy nor promiscuity was the dream implanted in their hearts as young children. Family life is what American children know and dream about and what they grow up wanting to be a part of. When our children become adults, their first desire is to establish a loving family with the person they have chosen to love.

We as American parents raise our children to want this. We as a so-ciety surround our growing children with images of families and ex-pect them as adults to live productive lives as active family members. Adults may grow distant from all their living relatives. But no matter how many friends we may have, it is still a sad event for us to lose our parents. And it is even sadder should all our family members pass away. We all need friends; but family relationships help make us feel that we are not alone in life.

If we say to our children that they cannot be married, or cannot start a new family which shares the bonds of love and memory with their childhood family, we break faith with them. We violate the dream we ourselves planted in their hearts. We raise our children to know who they are as part of a family; and if we withhold marriage and family from them, we rip apart the identity we gave them. Part of the implied promise which we as parents make to our children is the promise that they have the right to marry and extend the boundaries of our family. We promise to hand over to our adult children, and their marriage partner, the honor of taking over together as the new family heads. Our family becomes *their* family.

And when our children become adults, we look forward to having the honor of becoming a proud part of the family they now lead. Withholding the right to marry from our children violates the meaning and promise of family. Standing against Marriage Equality is a betrayal of America's children and is a direct attack on the American family. It is important for Christians who want to be pro-family to realize that this means standing in defense of civil Marriage Equality and Christian Marriage inclusivity.

IV. THE CHURCH NEEDS MORAL BOUNDARIES FOR CHRISTIAN MARRIAGE WHICH ARE BASED ON SCRIPTURE AND WHICH CAN INFORM ITS MINISTRY.

1. Examining the theological objections to civil Marriage Equality and Christian Marriage inclusivity demonstrates its faithfulness to Reformed teaching.

We've discussed some common social objections to enforcing Marriage Equality laws that are designed to extend civil marriage to same-sex couples. Now we need to address the two primary theological objections which arise from defining marriage inclusively as a commitment to love one person for a lifetime. 1) Divorce: If marriage is a lifetime commitment to love one person faithfully, is there room in a Christian's life for marriage to fail, or to become so destructive that keeping the commitment of marriage is worse than allowing divorce? 2) A Superior kind of marriage: Granted the first and only kind of scriptural example of marriage blessed by God is a faithful, procreative relationship between a man and a woman; are other patterns for faithful, loving, committed marriages somehow inferior, impure, not blessed by God or perhaps even sinful? We will examine both questions. Then, 3) We will briefly examine the doctrines of grace and sin which underlie our understanding of Christian Marriage and the moral boundaries defining it.

1. Divorce?

In the gospel of Matthew, chapter 19, verses 3 – 18, Jesus answers a question regarding marriage and divorce which was put to him by local Pharisees. Part of his answer is relevant here. Jesus "said to them, 'Because of your hardness of heart, Moses allowed you to divorce your wives, but from the beginning, it was not so'" (Matthew 19:8). Is Jesus telling us God is against all divorce?

As Reformed Christians, we might not say with Jesus that *hardness of heart* is the human problem bringing about the need for divorce. But we are realists about the sin which warps human society, human lives, and human relationships. In the light of this awareness, we have learned to make allowance for marriages that fail. We have learned to temper our moral guidance to married couples with our awareness that the presence of sin in human life means even well intended people will frequently fail to meet the demands of married love.

Even though we know Christian Marriage can sometimes demand more of us than we can give, it calls us to constantly strive to keep what we will call "the discipline of love." Within a marriage, our failures to follow the discipline of love can sometimes become great enough to inflict significant pain and damage on our mate. We learn from studying God's grace and mercy, that sometimes we need to let painfully failing marriages come to an end. Sometimes divorce is preferable to forcing people to endure the emotional and physical suffering that can be a part of a dying marriage.

For any number of reasons, it may be best to let people out of their promise to love a marriage partner for a lifetime. People who initially meant well may need to accept that their marriage has become destructive, and admit that they need to be given the chance to make a new beginning. The Reformed doctrine of grace needs to be understood as a message that God freely accepts us despite our failures, even when that failure involves a marriage in which we have both trespassed and been trespassed against. Maybe the trespassing in our marriage is not equal on both sides; but, in our best judgment, the marriage has become a toxic relationship.

Marriage may be a lifetime commitment to love one person faithfully. But it is only realistic to admit human love may fall short of what's needed to sustain the lifelong, creative, nurturing, and strengthening relationship marriage requires. Human failure is tragic. Divorce is almost always tragic. Divorce is a reason for feeling loss and grief. But it is not a life-ending sin. Our Reformed understanding of grace means we need to give Christians in failing marriages the chance to end that bad relationship and start anew. Our Reformed understanding of sin gives us every reason to expect that Christians may need multiple chances in any number of life's venues to fail and start anew. Divorce can be a much needed part of a Christian person's much needed new beginning.

2.   A Superior kind of marriage?

Natural superiority

A position I've heard taken in church discussions claims that procreative marriage between a man and a woman is the natural and therefore right form of marriage. This position is often based on what's known as "Natural Theology." Natural Theology points to what's happening in history and the physical universe, and on that basis, makes a judgment about God's intent and plan.

We have argued earlier in this Study Paper that procreative marriage has the ability to benefit and strengthen civil society. But is marriage between "one man and one woman" the only pattern providing society with a growing and productive population of workers? History would answer, "No." Biblical History gives the example of polygamy and presents it as a model of marriage which worked for its society. It didn't work perfectly; but neither does heterosexual monogamy. The one man and one woman pattern of marriage is simply not the only one able to meet the needs of society. The question remains, however, whether the Bible teaches that only the monogamous marriage of heterosexual couples is right or natural in God's sight.

I've previously made the point that all the biblical passages which prohibit sexual relations between same-sex couples are passages of Judicial law. They are all Civil or Judicial laws given to Moses by God solely for the purpose of governing Israel's life as a nation. Nothing in the Bible's Moral law covers same-sex marriage, or applies Moral law to just same-sex couples. Moral law requires married couples to be sexually faithful to each other. It requires married individuals to neither sexually use nor abuse their spouse, and to not treat their spouse as a possession whom they can use as an object of lust. This is what is morally right.

I suggest that nowhere does Scripture describe any behavior as "right by its nature." Humans were created to not sin. But it is no longer "in our nature" as humans to live sinlessly. A biblical argument might be made that it is now natural for humans to sin. But if the behavior natural to humans is sin, and heterosexual, procreative marriages are "natural," must we then pronounce them sinful? I suggest Scripture cannot be manipulated to support the notion that heterosexual, procreative marriages are either sinful *by nature*, or right and God-approved *by nature*.

If a marriage relationship between a man and woman is allowed to float naturally to its natural outcome, I suggest it's likely to drift towards producing two things: children and conflict. When procreative marriage is not seriously reinforced by hard work, good communication skills, patience, kindness, and able conflict resolution, it can naturally deteriorate into divorce and cause misery for the marriage partners and their children. Any successful marriage requires the couple to work hard to avoid the natural downward drift towards divorce.

There is no reason to claim heterosexual, procreative marriage is the one natural form of marriage. Perhaps one of the most painful consequences of this idea is that it slaps the label of "unnatural" on the marriages of sterile men and sterile women. How cruel! In addition, if the only procreative marriages are natural ones, then the marriages of older men and women who are past their childbearing years, also earn the label of "unnatural." Unnecessarily ageist, and also cruel! There is no *natural* reason to hold that heterosexual, procreative marriages are superior to same-sex or non-procreative marriages.

Scriptural superiority

Another argument for the superiority of heterosexual, procreative marriage attempts to base itself on Scripture. There is the Hebrews 13:4 Scripture argument. It's based on a mishandling of this passage in the King James Version of Scripture. Considering the increased availability in scriptural scholarship in the past few decades, it is not surprising we do not hear this argument much anymore. Still, let's give it its due. Secondly, there is the argument based on the role Adam and Eve play in Scripture. This argument has the apparent advantage that Jesus seems to champion it.

Argument One:

Marriage is honorable in all, and the bed undefiled; but whoremongers and adulterers God will judge. Hebrews 13:4 (KJV)

The King James Version translates the first half of this verse with verbal accuracy but not contextual accuracy. It uses words which individually correspond to the Hebrew text: "Marriage is honorable in all, and the bed undefiled." However, the rest of the sentence provides a context which necessitates a different translation than employed by the King James scholars. The sentence goes on to state in King James language, "but whoremongers and adulterers God will judge." The structure of the sentence takes the form of: "Do this; God will judge those who don't."

It is important, in this case, to distinguish between verbal and contextual accuracy. This important distinction dramatically changes the verse's meaning. *Do this* says the text: Treat marriage with honor by avoiding defilement. *Who defiles their marriage* according to the text: whoremongers and adulterers. *What will God do* according to the text: God will judge them.

By ignoring the implications of its grammatical context, the verse is wrongly interpreted (and consequently mistranslated by the King James scholars) to grant marriage an intrinsic honor, and give an intrinsic purity to married sex. This is not the intention of the text. Instead, the text of Hebrews challenges married couples to always treat their marriage with honor by keeping it undefiled by sexual sin. My own humble attempt at a better translation might be, "Marriage must be always held in honor, and married sex must be kept undefiled." The text explains how a couple dishonors and defiles their marriage. They dishonor and defile their marriage by engaging in sexual adultery, which it says, God will judge.

221

Clearly this Scripture does not unconditionally confer sanctity or God's blessing on marriage of any kind, either heterosexual or same-sex. The text challenges all married couples to maintain the honor and dignity of their marriages by avoiding sexual infidelity. The Hebrews 13 passage indirectly affirms what we have previously demonstrated: the moral defining line of marriage is sexual faithfulness.

Argument Two: The Adam and Eve pattern

> **And Pharisees came up to him [Jesus] and tested him by asking, "Is it lawful to divorce one's wife for any cause?" He [Jesus] answered, "Have you not read that he who created them from the beginning made them male and female, and said, 'Therefore a man shall leave his father and his mother and hold fast to his wife, and the two shall become one flesh'? So they are no longer two but one flesh. What therefore God has joined together, let not man separate." They said to him, "Why then did Moses command one to give a certificate of divorce and to send her away?" He [Jesus] said to them, "Because of your hardness of heart Moses allowed you to divorce your wives, but from the beginning it was not so. And I say to you: whoever divorces his wife, except for sexual immorality, and marries another, commits adultery." (Matthew 19: 3 – 9)**

A popular misinterpretation of this text claims that when Jesus quotes the Genesis chapter two passage, "Therefore, a man shall leave his father and his mother and hold fast to his wife, and the two shall become one flesh," he affirms that God's plan for marriage is for one man to marry one woman. The Matthew passage does not refer to Adam or Eve by name. But twice, in verses 4 and 8, Jesus refers to how marriage was, "from the beginning." In the book of beginnings, in the Genesis account which Jesus quotes, the couple being described, is in fact, Adam and Eve.

The problem with the "one man - one woman" interpretation is that the text clearly addresses only one thing: divorce. In verses 3 and 7, Jesus is asked about divorce. In verses 4 – 5, Jesus quotes from Genesis chapter two; in verse 8, he references the early history of divorce (presumably from Leviticus and Deuteronomy). In verses 6 and 9, Jesus states that he is answering questions about divorce. So, it is important to note that the passage in Matthew does not answer questions about how many are to be married, their gender, or their sexual orientation.

One of most common errors which leads to biblical misinterpretation arises from asking a question of the biblical text which it doesn't intend to address. The Matthew text intends to address the origin of divorce, making it clear divorce was not a part of God's original plan for marriage. Asking the Matthew text to answer questions apart from the origin of divorce is a mistake, and amounts to being unfaithful to the Scripture's intent.

Could we still conclude the marriage of Adam and Eve is a model for all future marriages, even if Matthew 19 doesn't give us the reason? We could, if another Scripture text elevated the marriage of Adam and Eve to a pattern for the rest of humanity. Is there such a text? Actually no. The Genesis 2 passage, which we have already discussed, describes marriage between a man and a woman; but as we pointed out, this description was meant to apply to the immediate descendants of Adam and Eve, and not to Adam and Eve themselves. Adam and Eve were in no position to leave their father or their mother before cleaving to each other. This injunction was undoubtedly recorded as though it were spoken to first couple in order to give it the greatest possible weight.

To consider what may be the actual marriage of Adam and Eve, we need to move forward to Genesis chapter three (Genesis 3:16 – 24). There, if we use our imagination, we may read an account of what could be the first couple's wedding. It is described in Genesis as being officiated by God shortly after Adam and Eve sinned. The ceremony consisted of several parts. God spoke to Eve and told her what her married role would be. God then spoke to Adam and told him what his married role would be. There was no modern exchange of rings to seal the marriage. There was instead the giving of a name; Adam gave his wife the name Eve. Then to consecrate the wedding, God killed animals; and with their skins, God provided new clothing to the now married couple. This service of marriage ended with one of the most dramatic benedictions or charges of all time. The Lord God sent the newlywed couple out of Eden, prevented their return, and charged them to go forth and till the ground, and to take up as a way of life the running of a working crop farm.

It only takes looking at a few passages to see that Scripture does not point to the marriage between Adam and Eve as an example for everyone to follow. Look nearby at the story of Cain and Abel in Genesis Chapter four.

> **Now Abel was a keeper of sheep, and Cain a worker of the ground. In the course of time Cain brought to the Lord an offering of the fruit of the ground, and Abel also brought of the firstborn of his flock and of their fat portions. And the Lord had regard for Abel and his offering, but for Cain and his offering he had no regard. (Genesis 4:2-5)**

This is a surprising passage. It purports to explain the origin of the longstanding cultural conflict, not only within Judaism, but within the ancient world, between crop farmers and shepherds. Adam was initially put in a garden and told to work and tend it. Then, when he and his wife were evicted from the garden, they were charged by God to continue living as farmers who tilled the soil. Cain followed his father's example, also planting and harvesting crops. In the ancient world, crop farmers lived a settled lifestyle, living near the fields they were cultivating, most likely forming small villages made of the families of fellow farmers.

According to the Genesis story, Abel took his own path, adopting a much different lifestyle than his father. Able raised sheep. In the ancient world, families who raised sheep did not live a settled village life; they lived as nomads. They traveled with the sheep from grassland to grassland, going where the sheep could graze and water. They were wanderers, a characteristic which came to be venerated by Israel as it looked back on its historical roots.

The hymn or chant in Deuteronomy which tells Israel's story, begins with the proclamation, "A wandering Aramean was my father" Deuteronomy 26:5. This wandering, nomadic lifestyle of "my father" became an idealized way of life among the Israelites. In the story of their history, they revered their early days as wandering nomads. They portrayed themselves as living closer to God in those days, because they had no cities (so could not make the mistake of Babel), and needed no ruler or king other than God.

This conflict between the settled farmer and the wandering sheep herder is played out in the story of Cain and Abel. Cain, who followed his father into crop farming, brought to God the fruits of his labor. Able who followed a different path, and became a nomadic sheep herder, also brought to God the fruit of his labor. Cain brought a sacrifice of fruits and vegetables and grains. Abel brought a sacrifice of a prized lamb. God approved of Abel's offering and of Abel himself – a good, pious nomad. God did not approve of Cain's offering, or of Cain – whose lifestyle as a settled crop farmer was morally suspect. In the mythos of Israelite history, God would be expected to approve of the nomad, and reject the settled farmer.

God's judgment on Cain is worth noting from the perspective of a nomad. Cain is cursed with no longer being able to farm and henceforth having to live as a wanderer (Genesis 4:12). And when Cain leaves God's presence, he "settles" in the land of "wandering, east of Eden" (Genesis 4:16). You might say God took this misguided farmer and straightened his life out by turning him into a wandering sheep herder like his dead brother had been. Not only did God straighten out Cain's lifestyle, but God also put a mark of protection on Cain, promising sevenfold vengeance from God on anyone who harmed Cain in his new nomadic way of life (Genesis 4:15).

The Genesis description of the first marriage fits a family of crop farmers: the man gives 24/7 to his fields; she births and raises their children. Adam and Eve, both in the Garden and after their eviction, farmed the soil and raised crops. Their one son who followed in his parents' footsteps became a murderer, and was forced by God off the farm and into a nomadic sheep tending lifestyle. The clear message of the Cain and Abel disaster was that a crop farming family did not meet with God's approval, a nomadic sheep herding family did.

However, if a farm wife's role as described in Genesis chapter three, is primarily to bear and raise children, we have to wonder what kind of farm she lived on. It must have been a very simple and primitive farm. Most of my aunts lived on farms; and their lives were as busy and as hard as the farm wife described in Proverbs 31. Today's farms are more mechanized, and the farm wife's job involves less doing by hand and less making from scratch, but the skill required and labor involved is just as significant. The Adam-and-Eve marriage pattern, consisting of a hardworking husband-farmer and a child raising wife, is clearly not held up in Scripture as applicable for all time or in all situations. Their own extended family followed many patterns. Among the descendants of Cain, were the father of all nomadic herders, the father of city builders, the father of musicians, and the father of those who forge iron and bronze (see: Genesis 4:17 – 22).

The point is that the marriage of Adam and Eve does not serve as a model for all the marriages that came after it. Marriage changes as the culture and economy that it exists within demands it change. Jesus points to the marriage of Adam and Eve to indicate that God did not originally intend divorce. Yet Christians today realize God's grace makes room for failures and new beginnings – even in marriage. As biblical Christians, we need to be sensitive to other ways that human nature, culture, and economy may require new ways of thinking about marriage. We need to be open to the rightness of civil Marriage Equality and Christian Marriage inclusivity in our current social context.

2. What does the rising social acceptance of Marriage Equality mean for the acceptance of marriage inclusivity within the Christian Church?

The LGBTQ (lesbian, gay, bisexual, transgender, queer or questioning) community has become increasingly vocal in expressing the desire of its members to share fully in the rights and responsibilities of marriage. The voice of this community needs to be recognized by society at large, not as a threat to family values, but as a clear victory for the core family values of Western culture, and for the family values of the Christian Church.

To understand the significance of the growing desire among the members of the LGBTQ community for the right to marry, it helps to realize that the desire to marry represents a massive change in values within the gay community since it initially "came out" at the 1969 Stonewall riots in Greenwich Village. I did not personally witness the emergence of gay culture and am in no position to write its social history. But as an aging child of the 60's, I can still recall the broad contours of the emerging gay culture from the late 60's and early 70's.

My early memories of gay culture include Bette Midler's TV comedy routines in which she talked about singing for gay men who gathered in Greenwich Village's bath houses. I also recall the defiant and sometimes angry mood of the first gay pride marches. I was young at the time. But I recall their robust counter-cultural spirit. The demonstrators expressed a determination to resist being crushed by the alienating forces of the American culture. The epithet "straight" stood for the condemnation of everything the gay community found oppressive in American culture.

These "liberated" gays announced they would not conform to the straight world and would be proud of not conforming. They defiantly proclaimed their disdain for straight society. They judged straight culture to be a negative influence with nothing to offer. Gay Pride was one among many counter-culture movements of that decade. But its hallmark goal was to denounce the stranglehold of straight culture. In addition, the early Gay Pride movement took up the spirit of sexual freedom and proudly stood for uninhibited promiscuity as symbolized by the bath house culture.

The song, "YMCA" was originally a defiant celebration of the "young men" involved in the gay culture of Greenwich Village. When the song came out in 1978, it originally proclaimed, "We are different; we are gay; accept us as we are!" The song has since lost most of its defiance. As it is performed today, everyone can sing along. Today it stands as a celebration of the uniqueness which makes each person special. But the attitude I recall being expressed by those early Gay Pride marchers was edgier, more rebellious and confrontational. They conveyed a righteous determination to reject the social conventions of straight morality which offered "one size fits all" rules that clearly did not fit them. Prior to 1973, straight society classified gay citizens as mentally ill, and incarcerated thousands of gay men and women in institutions, where many were given electroshock "therapy" or even lobotomized. Straight society not only did not fit the needs of its gay citizens; before 1973, it wasn't even safe for them.

I can recall nothing from the early Gay Pride movement that expressed a desire to join in a straight society which it considered corrupt. Their message was an in-your-face demand, "Accept us; accept gay culture." Standing as a sea change in gay culture, since the early days of Gay Pride, is the emergence of its new face with a new name: the LGBTQ or Rainbow Coalition. Participants in the LGBTQ movement have not maintained the earlier radical rejection of, and desire to overthrow, American social values. Instead, they have increasingly claimed the freedom promised by America's strong civil rights tradition to enable their active participation in the social, marital, and community life of America – the country which is theirs by birth.

Participants in the LGBTQ movement are declaring their readiness to fully join in American society; and they challenge it to live up to the social equality described in our nation's original statement of purpose: The Declaration of Independence. All people have equal rights, says the Declaration; not because our country recognizes human equality; but because equal rights are a birthright given by God to all humanity.

I hear it often said American society has made amazingly rapid progress in a very few decades towards accepting the rights of its gay citizens. That may be true, but America's gay citizens have made amazingly rapid progress in a very few decades towards accepting and championing the value of American marriage. The overwhelming embrace of marriage by the gay community represents a dramatic turnaround deserving of both note and credit.

I suggest it is amazing, given the hostility of so many American political leaders toward the rights of gay citizens, that so many gay couples today want to embrace the values represented by civil marriage. There are also large numbers of Christian men and women who are gay or lesbian and want to embrace the values represented by Christian Marriage. Today, these young men and women stand waiting for the Christian Church in which they were raised, whose faith they hold dear and live by, to claim them as the loyal sons and daughters they know themselves to be.

Today, the Christian Church is hearing the faith testimony of its gay sons and daughters. They are loyal to the Christian faith, even as their church excludes them from the fellowship of its families by denying them the membership right to seek Christian Marriage. These gay sons and daughters of the church find they cannot abandon the Christian faith, any more than they can abandon who they are, or the one they love. They strive to remain true to themselves, to their inner voice of faith in God, and to their inner voice of love. Can any Christian doubt the deep interconnectedness of the impulse to love and an active faith in God? This is one of the clearest messages in John's New Testament writings, in both his Gospel and his epistles.

We know there have been tragic moments in history when the Christian Church rejected its sons and daughters who held a firm faith, but who became unacceptable to the church because they stayed true to themselves or their convictions. They were judged "different," and the church declared them apostate or heretic or excommunicated. Many of these are sad moments which the church rightly desires not to repeat.

This is an appropriate time for the Christian Church to ask whether withholding marriage from gay Christians is a sad repetition of past moments when it mistakenly excluded other faithful Christians from its fellowship because it judged them to be different. On the other hand, it is appropriate to ask why, at this point in history, pressure is being put on Christian Churches to support Marriage Equality and marriage inclusivity; and why both equality and inclusivity for same-sex couples hasn't been the church's official stance throughout history.

We cannot infer from examining the historical development of Christian doctrine exactly what motivated the Church to hold a specific doctrine in a particular age and place. But we can make a general observation about how the Christian Church develops doctrine. The Apostle Paul and Augustine of Hippo are two instructive examples of key players in the history of doctrine. Neither man set out to write down every tenant of the Christian faith. Both men responded to the needs of the churches they served by answering the questions and addressing the problems brought to them.

The point is, Christian theology is situational by nature. This does not mean Christians make up their convictions as they go along. In every age, Christians base their beliefs on the study of Scripture and attempt to faithfully interpret the message of Scripture in a way that addresses the concerns of the world in which they live. The Scripture doesn't change. But Christians always develop theology to address the situations they face, and try to express that theology in language that speaks to their contemporaries. So although Christian Scripture stays the same, the way Christians hear its message changes in each age as they come to Scripture asking different questions. Our hope as Christians is that we continue to hear the timeless Word of God speaking to us through Scripture in a way that keeps the content of our message clear and the impact of our message fresh.

As the Christian church works to keep its marriage teaching both clear and fresh, it needs to recognize how the social changes now taking place around it require asking different questions of Scripture; and to ask itself whether the new insights arising from asking different questions are significant enough to require it to shift its understanding of marriage. The answer should be a clear, "Yes." There have been a few significant changes within our society unlike any the church has faced since its inception.

Same-sex love is far from new. But a confluence of forces in contemporary American culture has given rise to a new experience for gay people changing their relationship to society. Democratic idealism, Christian concern for social justice, the American civil rights movement, decriminalization of non-procreative sex acts, declassification of homosexuality as a mental illness, and a growing cultural awareness that the Christian message is one of acceptance and toleration for the dignity of all people, have acted together to give gay individuals a choice never before historically available. Contemporary American culture increasingly accepts its gay citizens and affords them the dignity of choosing to openly live together as loving, married couples.

For the first time in Western history, gay citizens are being allowed to shed the encumbrance of a furtive and duplicitous sexual life. Increasingly, unmarried gay individuals no longer need to pretend to be heterosexual or need to keep their loving, same-sex relationships hidden. Finding a life partner can be hard enough for anyone in the best of circumstances. But forcing gay people to hide their dating and

courtship under a shroud of secrecy surely adds unreasonable compli-
cation and pressure to a process that ought to be openly celebrated as
a wonderful part of life. Every society benefits from strong marriages.
Consequently, society is strengthened when it encourages its gay citizens to openly court and marry the people they love. In the same way,
society is weakened when it frustrates the efforts of its gay citizens to
find a marriage partner with whom they can build a loving marriage.

Increasingly, gay citizens have no need to enter into a mixed-orientation marriage (MOM), where they must create the false front of a
happy heterosexual marriage, living a lie damaging both spouses. Two
new possibilities have emerged that stand out as historically unique. It
is now possible for gay American citizens to consider a life of sexually
faithful, same-sex married love. It is also possible for gay American
citizens to openly speak out against and legally challenge the bullying
and terrorizing which has for too long kept gay individuals and couples hiding in closets of fear. In the past, it has been socially acceptable to savagely brutalize gay citizens. This abysmal behavior has not
been eradicated; but the legal approval it once received from society
is disappearing.

It is important for the Christian Church to recognize that the burgeon-
ing acceptance of gay individuals and gay love relationships does not
signify the moral degeneration of society. The Christian Church has
every reason to see this change, at least partially, as due to the success of its own message. The Church's preaching strongly emphasizes
God's loving acceptance of all people; and the church need not be surprised when the American society, which Christian preaching helped
form, exchanges an attitude of disdain towards the gay community for
the more Christian attitude of acceptance.

The message which the Christian church preaches is not only one of
acceptance; but particularly for the Reformed churches, it is also a
message of human dignity. In the Scott's Confession, human dignity is
described as the gift of God, who "created man . . . after his own im-

age and likeness." The dignity with which God endows humanity encompasses such qualities as: "wisdom, lordship, justice, free will, and self-consciousness." These remain human characteristics even though "man and woman both fell . . . from this dignity" (BoC 3.02).

Human dignity is not destroyed by the Fall. Human *wisdom* is demonstrated in its magnificence and fallibility by human culture. Human *lordship* is demonstrated in its magnificence and fallibility by human government. The magnificent yet fallible human awareness of *justice* is demonstrated by human legal systems. History does not provide a record of humans consistently using their *free will* to make good choices; but the magnificent scope of human creativity is undeniable. Human *self-consciousness* does not lead every human being to productive self-awareness; still, the human aptitude for self-reflection has produced magnificent philosophical and artistic achievements. The magnificent yet fallible quality of human dignity is in evidence everywhere in the human world. It is our heritage as beings created in God's image.

In Reformed teaching, dignity is not just an accident of human existence. It is a quality demanding recognition, and has both political and interpersonal consequences. The Westminster Confession discusses the political consequences of human dignity. It states that "civil magistrates" are "to protect the person and good name of all their people" from suffering any "violence, abuse or injury" against their dignity, especially the abuse of anyone's dignity predicated "upon pretense of religion" (BoC 6.129). The Westminster Larger Catechism discusses the interpersonal consequences of human dignity. It interestingly interprets the fifth commandment, "Honor your father and mother," as an injunction to show honor to those to whom honor is due. To our fellow citizens and fellow Christians, this means recognizing and honoring the fundamental "dignity and worth of each other in giving honor to" each other before ourselves, and rejoicing "in each other's gifts and advancement as . . . [though they were our] own" (BoC 7.241).

Dignity is a gift with which humans are created, and one which has both political and interpersonal consequences for Christian action. The church needs to recognize the moral demands of human dignity, and face with courage the ways in which it has failed to honor and protect the human dignity of its gay members. Will the Christian Church face and confess its culpability in helping to foster social conditions that have kept gay citizens from knowing the fulfillment of living their lives with a loving marriage partner? Will it find the courage to confess its culpability in encouraging countless sham mixed-orientation marriages (MOMs), in which the gay or lesbian partner has to pretend, almost always in public and sometimes even in private, to be straight? In these often tortured marriages, love is undermined by a lack of sexual/emotional desire on the part of one party and frustrated sexual/emotional desire on the part of the other. These marriages are sometimes further destroyed when their frustration expresses itself in secret or not-so-secret sexual betrayal. Will the church stand up and confess by singling out gay citizens for condemnation as sinners, when all human beings are equally guilty of sin in God's sight, it has given tacit permission for the deformation of countless marriages, as well as for countless misguided acts of violence against gay Americans?

Not only does the church need to take a stand in favor of Marriage Equality, the church needs to confess its role in driving gay men and women into faithless mixed-orientation marriages, its role in encouraging the brutalization of gay citizens by singling them out as being somehow more sinful than straight people, its role in withholding the blessing of married love and marital rights from gay couples, and its role in excluding Christian gay couples from the welcome and acceptance of the community of Christian families. When the church accepts its responsibility for doing real damage to the dignity of its gay sons and daughters, and violating the peace of church fellowship by marginalizing gay Christians, one can only pray it will gladly and boldly repent of these sins.

3. The Reformed Doctrine of Sin and Grace

Reformed pastors need not agree with every detail of Reformed confessional theology. However, as we review the Reformed doctrine of grace as expressed in the Reformed creeds, let us recognize the Reformed concept of grace emphasizes that the mercy God extends to sinful humanity. Our personal theologies might not exactly mirror the view of sin found in the Reformed creeds. But we do need to be faithful to the consequences of the fact, that within the Reformed creeds, the doctrine of sin is placed in the context of the doctrine of grace.

This is important because Reformed support for Marriage Equality and marriage inclusivity takes into account the grace of God, which challenges both partners in every marriage to embrace each other's strengths and accept each other's weaknesses *as freely as does God.* The Reformed view of God's grace provides a unique and transformative way of understanding human life. By placing the concept of sin within the context of grace, Reformed teaching allows sin to be treated as a tool for labeling, exposing, and managing those behaviors and attitudes that erode relationships. It allows marriage partners to both face and forgive the sin in themselves and their marriage. It also challenges married couples to deal with the fact the sin in their lives often makes their best attempts at love for each other fall short.

Grace allows Christians to face the pervasive and corrosive impact of sin on all aspects of human life (their own and their loved ones' lives) without their psyches being weighed down with the burden of guilt or shame. God's grace allows sin and its destructive impact to be admitted openly to ourselves and to all with whom we share an intimate relationship, including God. The power of God's grace does not eliminate sin from the life of Christians; instead, grace offers an accepting environment within which our destructive impulses can be openly confessed, and exposed to the healing and transformative influence of human and divine love. We cannot expect grace and love to heal our every sinful impulse. We cannot expect grace and love to so transform us that we never hurt another person, or to make us so strong and secure we are never allow ourselves to be hurt. What God's grace does is allow us to honestly face and creatively deal with the hurt we have inflicted and sustained.

The Reformed doctrine of human sin isn't supposed to be a club used to beat people down with guilt and shame. It is supposed to be a freeing message, a component of our message about God's gracious acceptance of humanity in its weakness and brokenness. And it is supposed to teach us to accept ourselves, forgive each other, and take people as they are – broken and in need of all the love we can give them. It is this attitude, based on the Reformed doctrine of sin, seen through the doctrine of grace, which we need to bring to a Christian understanding of Marriage Equality and marriage inclusivity.

At this point, it will be useful to briefly sketch the outline of the Reformed doctrines of grace and sin and indicate how they provide an essential background for understanding the way in which both equality and inclusivity fit into a Reformed understanding of Christian Marriage.

Grace is the beginning point of Reformed theology. Reformed theology holds that for all of human history, God's every outreach to humanity has been an expression the Gospel of Jesus Christ (BoC 4.018 – 4.019). Said another way, grace describes God's every dealing with humanity, from our first step outside of the Garden of Eden until this very moment (BoC 6.039). Reformed theology understands God as a God of grace, and the Reformed doctrine of sin can only be understood in the bright light of the God's grace.

However, despite this strong emphasis on grace, awareness of sin is described by the first generation reformer, Heinrich Bullinger, as a miserable experience. In the Second Helvetic Confession, written by Bullinger in 1561, he states a sinful person should have "a feeling of shame" over which he or she "grieves" (BoC 5.093). Bullinger further describes this misery by saying when sinners "come to know the truth" about their sin, they lament, weeping bitterly, and bewailing their sin with tears (BoC 5.094). This awful, shame ridden awareness of sin is not currently a part of Reformed theology. Repentance is no longer described as feeling miserable and wretched about our sin; neither need it involve the toxic attitudes of shame or guilt.

A century after the Second Helvetic Confession was written, in the early heyday of English Presbyterianism, sin was defined as violating the moral law. The Westminster Confession of Faith of 1647 described "sin, as contrary to the holy nature of . . . God" and "the righteous law of God" (BoC 6.082). Following this law-based understanding of sin, the British, the Scottish, and the American Presbyterian Books of Worship (up to and including the 1946, American, "Book of Common Worship"), encouraged believers to stimulate their awareness of sin in preparation for receiving Holy Communion by meditating on the Ten Commandments, the codification of the Moral Law (BoC 7.041). These Presbyterian books of worship directed believers to confess having broken each of the Ten Commandments. The point of defining sin as breaking the Ten Commandments was to establish that sin is *limited to* violating these ten moral laws and that the human conscience should be free from the burden of any other added *made up laws*.

The use of the Ten Commandments to define sin within the English Reformed tradition had the original intent of bolstering Christian Liberty and enforcing the Liberty of Christian Conscience (BoC 6.109). The Westminster Confession describes Christian Liberty as the insistence that Christians must not have their consciences bound by the false duty to obey *made up* moral rules which are contrary to or other than the ten moral laws contained in Scripture. The Westminster Confession described these *pseudo moral laws*, no matter how wise sounding they might be, whether made up by either religion or borrowed from society, to be mere "commandments of men," which God has left Christians free to not obey. In the Reformed theology of the Westminster era, one of the most important commands, which Christians are to take seriously, is God's insistence that we not add any rules of our own to God's moral law (BoC 5.082; 6.006).

The doctrine of Christian Liberty in Reformed creedal theology, expresses the awareness that when humans get involved in religious life, we are likely to add lots of *moral-sounding rules* we can check off as we achieve them, in order to demonstrate to ourselves and to others that we are good religious people. Christian Liberty insists that the Christian conscience must be left free from these *made-up* laws. Contemporary Christian denominations enforce any number of these *made-up* laws regarding marriage. Reformed theology holds that the Christian conscience is free from those marriage laws made up by religions and not found in the Ten Commandments. As demonstrated earlier, Christians who define Christian Marriage with careful attention to the guidance of the Ten Commandments, end up with solid support for both civil Marriage Equality and Christian Marriage inclusivity.

As we come to the contemporary Presbyterian Creeds, we find them abandoning a law-based understanding of human sin. Increasingly, contemporary Reformed confessions emphasize that we humans become aware of our sin in the light of God's mercy, and as we confront how our love falls short of the gracious, saving love of Jesus Christ. The theology of the Contemporary Reformed creeds affirms that our experience of God's gracious, merciful love moves us to embrace God in faith and trust.

The Confession of '67 makes this point quite strongly. The wording of this modern confession states that we become aware of the sin in our lives as we face the reality of "the reconciling act of God in Jesus Christ (BoC 9.12)." It is not looking on God's law that causes us to see our sinfulness; it is the standard of "God's love in Jesus Christ" shedding the light of God's judgment on our lives, revealing "all human virtue" to be sin which is "infected by self-interest and hostility" (BoC 9.13). God's love does not bring down on us the crushing experience of guilt and shame. Instead, God's love frees us to experience a repentance which trusts God and finds new life in Christ (BoC 9.14)

A major function of the Reformed doctrine of sin throughout these different eras is to prevent humans from hiding behind the pretense of either moral competence or moral superiority. It becomes essential then, to a Reformed understanding of Christian Marriage, that partners learn to drop the masks of moral competence and moral superiority with each other. Consider that the primary moral requirement of marriage is sexual faithfulness as described in the Ten Commandments, and that Jesus' definition of sexual faithfulness denies the human ability to achieve it by equating sexual lust (a common if not universal human experience), with sexual adultery (Matthew 5:27 - 28).

The Reformed understanding of Christian Marriage begins with the realistic and freeing assumption that nobody plays the role of marriage partner right. Nobody gets to claim their marriage or their part in it is morally unimpeachable in God's sight; but nobody has to. Christian Marriage is a relationship all about love, something we humans all fail at in any number of ways. The good news of God's grace is that God accepts us as sinful, broken, and fallible. Christian Marriage is designed for sinful humans who want to try to love one particular sinful and broken person faithfully for a lifetime (W 4.8001). Reformed theology holds that both same-sex and opposite-sex couples who marry will fall short of a Christ-like love for each other. Marriage equality simply means that any Christian couple who wants to undertake the *impossible* challenge to love with a Christ-like love one person faithfully ought to have an equal chance to try.

A brief but deeper look into the Reformed doctrine of sin will illuminate the equal moral standing before God of same-sex and opposite-sex couples. To make this clear, we need to highlight the Reformed distinction between sin and sin*s*.

FIRST: Sin. In Reformed Creedal theology, sin is first and foremost a matter of human nature (BoC 3.03; 4.005; 6.035). Our nature is itself corrupted by sin (BoC 5.037). Our desires are "adverse to all good" (BoC 5.037); and are "prone to all that is evil" (BoC 4.060). Sin causes every person to "lose their humanity" (BoC 9.12); a loss which wholly defiles "all the faculties and parts of soul and body" (BoC 6.32). Humanity is not devoid of goodness and dignity; the image of God in humanity is not erased by sin. But every mental, emotional, and physical "faculty" of our humanity is eroded by sin's touch.

As a consequence, every marriage involves two flawed people. Every couple, same-sex or opposite-sex, consists of two broken people trying their best to meet the impossibly demanding challenge of married love. Marriage Equality and marriage inclusivity both need to be mor-ally honest. Reformed theology recognizes that all couples who come to either civil marriage or Christian Marriage are equally disadvantaged by sin. Christians who have suggested that same-sex couples are living in sin while opposite-sex couples are not, do not understand the problem of human sin. Sin touches and undermines every aspect of everyone's humanity. Even our best and most admirable attempts at goodness and love are infected with sin (BoC 9.13). The Reformed doctrine of sin places all couples seeking marriage on an equal moral footing.

SECOND: Sins. In Reformed Creedal theology, sin-corrupted human nature is the cause of all "actual sins" or "actual transgressions" (BoC 6.034). Sin is a condition; sins are actions. These actions or "sins are not equal;" "some are more serious than others" (BoC 5.039). Some sinful actions cause more destruction to their perpetrators and victims, some cause less (BoC 7.083). Still, no one gets to boast that their sins are not serious; no matter how small the transgression; every sinful act "deserves damnation" (BoC 6.084; 7.084).

The point of the Reformed doctrine of <u>sins</u> is to be realistic about the wide range of human misdoings. It recognizes humans are capable of trivial wrongdoing and epically destructive wrongdoing. Probably most human lives are spent doing neither great evil nor great good. But the Reformed doctrine of <u>sin</u> is the great leveler. The Reformed doctrine of sin makes it clear that whether your sins are small or large, they are equally spiritually deadly. The Confession of '67 is eloquent on this point. It reads,

> All men, good and bad alike, are in the wrong before God and helpless without his forgiveness. Thus all men fall under God's judgment. No one is more subject to that judgment than the man who assumes that he is guiltless before God or morally superior to others" (BoC 9.13).

No one gets to be morally superior. Reformed theology has a doctrine of sin leading directly to Marriage Equality by giving equal moral standing to all couples seeking marriage.

Let Reformed Christian pastors, who desire to give good spiritual care to the Christian men and women who come to them, be careful to act as skilled workmen, able to accurately interpret the word of truth (II Timothy 2:15). As Reformed pastors teach Scripture, let us allow the Reformed Creeds to guide us toward a correct interpretation of Christian Marriage. It is not acceptable for the Reformed Churches to use the voice of Scripture to defend a popular cultural bias against same-sex marriage. When the Church knows it has correctly interpreted the guidance of Scripture, and faithfully understood the meaning of Christian Marriage, let the Church boldly teach the message of civil Marriage Equality and Christian Marriage inclusivity, and no other.

WORKS CITED

In Sections One, Two, and Three of *Preparing for Christian Marriage*

Book of Confessions (BoC). Louisville: Office of the General Assembly, The Presbyterian Church (USA), 1999. Web. May 2000.

Calvin, John, *The Institutes of the Christian Religion*. Trans. by John. T. McNeill, Ed. Philadelphia: The Westminster Press, 1960. Print.

The Holy Bible, *Contemporary English Version®* (CEV®). New York: American Bible Society, 1995. Print.

> (Several times the *Contemporary English Version* of the Bible is cited because of its superior ability to render the original biblical languages in clear English sentences.)

Directory for Worship (W). Louisville: Office of the General Assembly, The Presbyterian Church (USA), 2015 – 2017. Web. June, 2015.

The Holy Bible, *English Standard Version®* (ESV®). Wheaton: Good News Publishers, 2001. Web. August, 2013.

> (The *English Standard Version* of the Bible is the primary version used throughout all three parts of *Preparing for Christian Marriage*. It is an excellent and faithful modern translation. If a short phrase from a passage of Scripture is quoted without attribution in the course of discussing the larger passage, the quoted words are taken from the ESV.)

The academic apparatus employed in this document follows the general guidelines for textual notes which is appropriate to a topical essay. It also employs certain aspects of footnote format, which is appropriate to theological discourse, so greater specificity in documentation is possible. The use of academic apparatus is consistent throughout to make it easier for readers to use.

ABOUT THE AUTHOR:

Steve Wigall is an ordained Presbyterian pastor, teacher, writer, and spiritual director, honorably retired from the Presbytery of Northern New England.

Steve has devoted a major part of his pastoral ministry to the nurture and training of Christian couples. He also spent over a decade involved in the leadership of the ministry of Presbyterian Marriage Encounter – an organization that focuses on the strengthening and enrichment of Christian Marriage. Those years of experience are reflected in this book.

Steve was born in Lindsay, California on April the 15th, 1951 and was married in 1974. He graduated from the University of California at Santa Cruz, earning an AB in Religion in 1972, and obtained a State Certificate in Elementary Education & Social Science from California State University-Bakersfield in 1973. From September 1974 to May 1977 he studied for and earned his master of divinity at Princeton Theological Seminary in NJ; then in 1978, he earned a postgraduate master's in Homiletics and Historical Theology, also from Princeton Theological Seminary.

From August 1985 to May 1987, Steve studied and obtained a Certificate in Spiritual Guidance from the Guild for Spiritual Guidance - Wainwright House, Rye, NY. The program involved training in group and individual Spiritual Guidance, and included the study of the History of Christian Spirituality and Jungian Psychology. From 1989 to 1998, Steve continued studying both Christian Spirituality and Psychology at Boston University School of Theology, earning a dual emphasis Doctorate of Theology.

His pastoral career started at the United Presbyterian Church of Millstone, NJ, where he worked from January 1978 to January 1987, developing his skills in preaching, teaching, counseling, leadership training, administration, and fellowship building.

In 1990, he assumed the position of pastor of St. Andrew's Presbyterian Church, Kennebunkport, ME, continuing to use his skills in leadership training to help build this young congregation. His teaching career included working from 1993 to 1997 at the Northern Essex Community College where he developed and taught courses in World Religions, Psychology, Acupressure, and Yoga.

Steve's wide-ranging religious and spiritual knowledge and training have enabled him over the years to concentrate on offering both individual and small group spiritual direction. In 1995, Steve initiated a Spiritual Direction ministry named Spiritual Compass. At the same time, he began serving as Parish Associate at Eliot Presbyterian Church, Lowell MA. He continued this volunteer work until phasing it out in about 2010.

Steve further brings Jin Shin Do acupressure training to his work, which speaks to his conviction that Spirit / Body interface and interaction are essential to a healthy Christian spiritual life. He strives to help his clients work toward spiritual, mental, emotional, and physical wholeness as individuals, as married couples, as family members, and as active members of their communities.

Steve currently makes his skills available as a resource to the ELCA Lutheran church where he is active as a volunteer in Andover, MA; and to the ministry of the Gay Christian Network (GCN: gaychristian.net) where he volunteers as a General Moderator on their blog site.

Publications:

A Sacramental Paradigm Employing the Lord's Supper in Calvin as a Theological Rationale for Spiritual Direction (1998); "What Is a Spiritual Director's Authority?" (1997); "History's Role in Defining Spiritual Direction." (1998).

Contact Information: uncwigg@yahoo.com